Praise

'Here is a "greatest hits" album for people who want to sample a broad spectrum of sales knowledge. Jamie Hamer's album might be entitled, *The Essential Sales Collection*, or *Best of Sales and Selling*. He has painstakingly organised interviews with top sales professionals by category and even highlighted the best bits for the reader. I know many of the interviewees well, and they are serious sales contenders. These are truly exceptional sales career insights – the "greatest hits" – a smart starting place for anyone interested in becoming a sales professional or a seasoned salesperson who wants to stay sharp and keep growing.

   — **Lee McCroskey**, speaker, trainer and coach, Southwestern Speakers and the John Maxwell Team

'Read *The Exceptional Sales Career* and you'll find practical, seasoned wisdom from sales veterans from across the business spectrum. The strength of this book is that the author has painstakingly sorted through hundreds of hours of interviews he has conducted with topflight sales professionals and arranged them into 100 lessons that salespeople will most certainly face in their careers. Its content is rich, so my advice would be to "drip read" sections each day and then put them into practice. Undoubtedly, consuming and acting on these

principles and practices will lead to a successful
sales career.'
— **Scott Roy**, CEO and co-founder, Whitten &
Roy Partnership

'Jamie Hamer's book is a cornucopia of wisdom
for those who are considering a career in sales. It
highlights, by way of various anecdotes and quotes,
how to become a star performer instead of an "also-
ran". I was delighted to be asked to contribute to the
publication, which will undoubtedly become a bible
for all sales novices.'
— **Jeremy Jacobs**, speaker and conference
presenter, The Sales Rainmaker®

'A book with actionable advice is a must-have when
you're in sales. This powerful book, full of real-life
advice and examples from sales leaders around the
globe, gives us a sneak peek into the world of sales.
I especially appreciate the openness and storytelling
skill of all the interviewees.'
— **Hans Keijmel**, Strategic Account Director,
Bloomreach

'Many of the nuggets in this book are familiar; others are new. We can never know all the answers, but being reminded that sales is a service, that today we need to be agile, and that we won't always get it right, is priceless. In these uncertain times, delivering results alongside others is paramount, and the need for reverting back to processes that work, along with being in tune with the "why", really hits home.'

— **Rupa Datta**, Owner, Portfolio People

THE EXCEPTIONAL SALES CAREER

100 Key Lessons
from Sales Leaders
to Ensure
Selling Success

Jamie Hamer

Rethink

First published in Great Britain in 2021
by Rethink Press (www.rethinkpress.com)

Cover image © Shutterstock | Libellule

Contents

Introduction

Like most projects with a salesperson masquerading as a project manager, this project went massively over in terms of time and budget. The truth is, I only intended to write a book about the lessons I had learned over my twelve-year sales career, lessons that I would have wanted my twenty-year-old self to know – many of which are expressed in this book, only more eloquently through the words of others. I wrote a short book about my own experiences, started interviewing the people who I had met upon the way, until I was introduced to people who I hadn't met previously, but whom it would have been criminal not to interview. Soon, the project turned into curation of the best wisdom I could find, to the point where my own insights were secondary to the wisdom of over 2,000 years of sales experience.

Ultimately, a lot of the lessons in the book were ones I learned (or relearned) myself throughout the process. It became evident the maths of sales (lesson 60) was important, as I approached more than 250 people to find a brilliant 105 interviewees. Much like any sales pipelines, the 'noes' (or non-answers) were as essential as the 'yeses' (lessons 12 and 75). By the end of the process, I was working purely on referrals (lesson 98), which increased the interview quality further. But I was certainly always selling (lesson 36), with interviewees coming from recommendations from my parents, spouses referring each other, workmates, fellow Toastmasters,[1] friends and relatives, and even a gentleman I met on the Eurostar from London to Paris.

I also learned, as I have learned many times before, that as a salesperson I have an enormous propensity to buy (lesson 7). Along the way, I read a number of books that were suggested by interviewees, I bought a selection of high-end vitamins, I almost invested in a Bulgarian tourist attraction, I employed someone, and I am likely to invest in two UK-based startups as a result of the conversations I had on this journey.

In terms of the interviewees, this book will naturally be flavoured by my own experience, and the network I have relied on for their expertise and wisdom. The most formative of my experiences as a salesperson was selling educational books door-to-door with Southwestern Advantage[2] – a programme where over 3,000 young adults typically converge on Nashville,

---

1   www.toastmasters.org
2   www.southwesternadvantage.com

Tennessee, for an intensive week-long sales training before working as independent contractors for the summer. You work eighty hours per week on pure commission, selling educational books door-to-door. It's a wonderfully difficult programme that creates a strong bond between all that experience it. Of my interviewees, 37% 'sold books', which gives this book a strong flavour of the time-honoured sales principles we were all taught there. Those individuals have gone on to be wildly successful in a wide variety of fields.

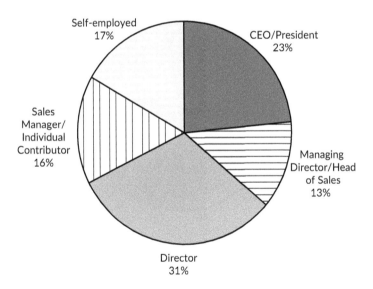

Interviewee role

There may be some lack of diversity in the book, though none of it intentional. 26% of my interviewees were women, which unfortunately is not quite representative of even the tech or finance industry, an issue I apologise for. Without trying to sound too much like a politician, there was plenty of diversity in terms of role (as shown in the figure above), age, sector (as shown in the figure below) and personality type. The unifying theme is that they are all on the top of their game, whether in sales directly or in wider business leadership.

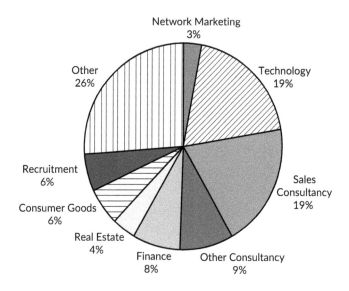

Interviewee sector

To give some insight into the process itself, I tended to ask these questions to every interviewee:

- What have you found most fulfilling about your sales career thus far?

- What's the best thing about being in sales?
  The worst?

- What's the best thing about your industry?
  The worst?

- What is the biggest difference between successful
  and unsuccessful salespeople?

- What additional skills are needed to succeed in
  your industry?

- What elements of culture make a sales organisation successful?

- What advice would you give to aspiring
  salespeople?

- If you were starting your sales career again, what
  would you do differently?

- Can you tell me about a time you failed to make a
  sale and learned something valuable?

- Can you tell me about a time you succeeded
  in selling and it showed off the skills you've
  developed?

For the outline of these thought-provoking questions
I am grateful to the book *Power Questions* by Andrew
Sobel and Jerold Paras,[3] which was recommended
to me by my primary sales mentor, Theo Davies of

---

3 A Sobel and J Paras, *Power Questions: Build relationships, win new
business, and influence others* (Brilliance Corporation, 2013)

Google, whose wisdom is well represented in this book.

Lastly, I should caution that there may be some overlap in these lessons, which is a good thing. Different expressions of the same principles can resonate with different people, and my aim was to get as many powerful quotes into this book as I could possibly justify.

Ultimately, I hope my twenty-year-old self would have taken some concrete, actionable learnings from these lessons, and I hope they are also massively helpful as a means towards building your own exceptional sales career.

1
Should You Go Into Sales?

'You have to believe that you are going to be successful, or you shouldn't jump into sales. Look at who makes the most money in sales; when you think about what they do, do you just get completely deflated? If so, maybe choose another career. However, if you think, "I'm happy to work for it. I'm going to enjoy it. I believe I can make a difference and I believe I can make money," then go into sales.'
— John Schlegel, Chief Executive Officer (CEO),
   Stonebridge Search

Lesson 1: Ask why, and why again

Get to the deeper why

It was 8pm and I had knocked on fewer than sixty doors, with no hope of hitting my allotted target. It was a cool, neutral evening with not a person in sight. I started to cry for the first time that I could remember. As I began to taste salt, I sat on the edge of a suburban street corner in dusty Colorado Springs, USA, questioning how I had ended up there.

The simple explanation was that I was expected to knock on a hundred doors that day, selling educational books to parents with school-aged kids. I had decided to travel over 4,500 miles to be an independent contractor, selling door-to-door in the USA on straight commission for the summer.

I remembered my resilience training, provided the previous week, and I leaned into the 'productive thoughts' I had stored for this occasion. I envisioned my dad in front of me saying, as he had many times before, 'Whatever happens, Jamie, do what you say you're going to do.' I got up, and I knocked on fifteen more doors before night fell. Seventy-five wasn't one hundred, but it was a start.

Deciding you want to be in sales is a big choice. While a sales career can be brilliant, there are significant downsides to the profession (as explored in Chapter 2: Sales Downsides) and 51% of salespeople regularly fail to achieve their targets.[4]

The journey of understanding *whether* you should be in sales begins with the search for *why* you should. Simon Ruddick, Chairman, Albourne Partners, recommends:

'Lock yourself in a dark room and put a moist towelette on your head. In the moment of deepest

---

4   C Brown, '50% of salespeople fail to achieve their targets!' (ISM, 2017), https://blog.bridgegroupinc.com/inside-sales-metrics, accessed 6 November 2020

internal candour you're capable of, figure out what scoreboard internally drives you and what adventure you want to have.'

Raf Tristao, Head of Strategic Accounts, HG Insights, recalls a recruitment day:

'I saw a bunch of people giving presentations about why they want to be in sales. There were a few where their heart really wasn't in it. They were saying the things that they had been coached to say, which manifests through your enthusiasm and through your body language. It is important to dig into the real motivators. Everything starts with motivation and that's what's going to drive you on a cold winter morning, when it's raining and you have a two-hour commute and you're not feeling too well. What is going to motivate you to look at it and say, "I'm going to have a great day at work, and just smash it?"'

A common technique to dig deeper is to 'ladder' five whys to get to your root cause, which needs to be strong enough to motivate you through really hard times ahead.[5]

---

5   It's believed that the 'Five Whys' technique was developed by Sakichi Toyoda, the Japanese industrialist, in the 1930s. For more, see 'Origins of the 5 Whys technique' (Mindtools, no date), www.mindtools.com/pages/article/newTMC_5W.htm, accessed 16 November 2020.

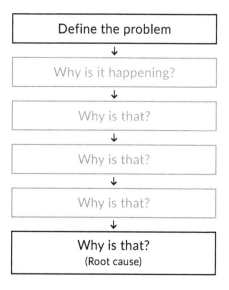

The Five Whys

Slim Earle of The Chemistry Group recommends this:

> 'It's the laddering technique of why, why, why that will get you to true intent. At the surface level, I might say I did something to build a relationship, but "why" might actually be because I need that relationship to get my commission.'

Self-searching is crucial

Manny Gonzalez, Financial Advisor, Raymond James, shares his unique motivations:

'I would recommend reverse-engineering it: "What kind of lifestyle do I want for me and my family?" I'm from Mexico. I was six years old when we came here. My parents worked at a jewellery company – a traditional nine-to-five job. I was never hungry, I wasn't poor, but when I saw my buddy's dad that was at every single practice, at every single game, always present and always available for his kid; and also had a great lifestyle, had money, freedom, time and had a good house – that's what I wanted. I wanted that time, I wanted that freedom, I wanted the money and I wanted a legacy for my kids. So I said, "What can I do to have that?" Sales provided that vehicle where I could have that, and then I said, "OK, what am I really good at?" It was relationships. I love helping people. "So, what career path out there can I be in sales that I can help people and work with people?" That's how I fell into financial planning.'

KEY TAKEAWAY

As we will see throughout this book, you can make any combination of age, personality traits and circumstance work in sales, as long as you have that strong 'why' in place. Make sure you have it firmly in grasp before taking the plunge.

Lesson 2: Introvert vs extrovert matters

The typical view

Of the interviewees, more than 80% of those who volunteered an answer suggested that extroverts were better suited for sales, though many did so with caveats. Mark Cooper, Owner, Cooper and Lansbury Associates, is one example:

> 'I think extraversion helps if you look at these types on any sort of personality scale. Those people who get their energy from being with others and from networking can go into a sale and feel confident about it. However, what I've learned along the way is that those who really don't want to be salespeople actually tend to be quite good at it because they aren't "salesy", in inverted commas.'

Introvert successes

However, there are plenty of counterexamples, including Kristen Gonzalez, VIP Brand Promoter, Thrive, a top network sales professional who struggled at first:

> 'Back in college when I heard about a sales internship, I was a communications major but I was actually very shy. I hated to order pizza because I didn't want to talk to people on the phone. I hate being in McDonald's, going up and ordering my meal. I just didn't like talking to people. I knew I needed to do something to get over that fear, because in

life, I was going to have to deal with people no matter what I did.'

Slim Earle of The Chemistry Group shares his observations of introverted salespeople:

'We worked with a pharmaceutical company, and all of their highest performing salespeople are introverts, which did not fit the hypothesis of their senior stakeholders. They were field-based salespeople selling to pharmacists. Pharmacists have a physical barrier between them and the rest of the world in pharmacies, so the naturally introverted people had a better level of interaction and engagement from a typically introverted pharmacist. The company led with content and commercials, which is what made them high-performing in that context. If you put them in a telecoms company, then extraversion becomes quite a critical piece because you are interacting with senior business leaders, and you need to be excited and energised. There is subtlety in the specific sales environment.'

Matching your audience

Stuart Lotherington, Managing Director (MD), SBR Consulting, explains:

'What most people think if they say, "Oh, you would make a good salesperson," is someone who does a lot of talking, somebody who is expressive and lights up a room. This is not a good test at all. I had the lucky opportunity to be a judge on the UK National Sales Awards a few years ago where there were ten finalists that I had to interview. What I found fascinating was that they all seemed to be reflective of the personalities they were selling to. I have also found with the businesses that I have worked with that the highest performers seem to be the ones that reflect their clients the most, whether that is learned or whether that is natural.'

KEY TAKEAWAY

It seems likely that either introversion or extraversion – or indeed any personality type – can work in the right environment. Success depends more on the skillset and practice needed to adapt your communication style (lesson 65) and needed to own your industry (lesson 94), where you should look for similarities in terms of personality type with those whom you engage with and sell to.

Lesson 3: You need ego and empathy

The need for ego, but not too much

According to an article in the *Harvard Business Review*,[6] the typical top-performing salesperson requires a high

---

6   D Mayer and H Greenberg, 'What makes a good salesman', *Harvard Business* Review (2006), https://hbr.org/2006/07/what-makes-a-good-salesman, accessed 7 September 2020

level of empathy, without sympathy, and a high level of ego, without dominance. I've heard it described as an 8/10 on each, which dovetails well with the results of my interviews and experience.

Theo Davies, Head of Cloud Sales Enablement JAPAC, Google, says:

> 'The most successful salespeople naturally, and surprisingly, are actually very selfish. It's what makes many people good at sales – number one, they're hungry. They're go-getters. They love the recognition. It's actually the same reason many salespeople do not make good managers and great managers generally aren't very good at selling. It's very rare that you get someone who's good at both. What tends to be the dividing factor is the ability to, or really the desire to, help others at the expense of yourself.'

Eric Hirschberg, CEO, Echo Finance, describes a salesperson who took ego too far:

> 'He wasn't reading people's body language. These are people who were incapable of saying "no" to him. He was wasting his time with multiple meetings on something that was not going to happen, and he never really got to the point of figuring out what their objections were or why it wasn't going to happen. It was all about his ego.'

Mike Turner, MD, YouBecome Consulting, makes a suggestion:

'One good habit is to ask for help, and not have an ego which is so massive that you'll say, "No, I can do it by myself." Well, sometimes you might need someone to watch you do it. Because you might have got yourself into a bad habit that you may not realise you're doing.'

The need for empathy, but not too much

Ron Alford, Senior Partner, Southwestern Consulting, describes an ideal salesperson:

'For me an ideal person in sales is someone that understands themselves; they really understand their qualities and are authentically themselves, but they've got emotional intelligence to read the person they're with and be a chameleon. They'll kick it up a little bit when there's an energetic person there with them and be visually engaged. Then sometimes when it's someone that's soft-spoken and logical, they can turn it down a notch. It's the personality that is not locked into one thing, it's able to adapt, that's strongest.'

For empaths, losing a sale can be especially hard. Connie Smith, Consultant, Whitten & Roy Partnership, remembers such a sale:

'I felt extremely disheartened as I had formed relationships with the sales leadership and wanted to help an organisation which was doing so much good. I could put myself in their situation and wanted to help them solve it. Being an empathetic salesperson is a double-edged sword. The lesson that I took from that is not to waste my time with the wrong people. I reminded myself that although I love my job and I am helping people, it is a sale and therefore I need to be as efficient about that as possible.'

KEY TAKEAWAY

If you find yourself with ideal amounts of both empathy and ego, then sales would definitely be a good fit for you. If you're not at the ideal 8/10 range, then all is not lost – I started my career at about 9/10 on ego and 6/10 on empathy, and have consciously aimed to balance the two. You can choose to focus on your determination (lesson 91) or to focus on others (lesson 85), but a fairly high level of ego and empathy to start in sales is a must.

Lesson 4: You need resilience

Resilience is a key factor

When I asked interviewees what the biggest difference between successful and unsuccessful salespeople was, the number one answer was that successful people possessed grit, resilience or tenacity.

Ron Alford, Senior Partner, SBR Consulting, says that this difference is critical:

'The bounce-back factor – being able to be resilient – it's like a muscle that has to be exercised. When I have a setback or a failure or a "no" or even when I'm rocking for a week, if I sit there and dwell on it or think about it or take my foot off the gas or over-analyse it, it's goodnight. I'm going to struggle. When I can bounce back quickly and learn from it and just say, "Cool, who's next?" I have the ability to overcome anything.'

Ilias Vartholomaios, CEO, Owiwi, a game-based personality test provider, agrees with this sentiment:

'We have found the soft skill of resilience to be relevant across all sales positions. We define this ability not only in terms of how much you can "take" in terms of pressure but also how quickly and well you'll recover from setbacks – because you will suffer setbacks in sales. Working in sales, having strong resilience is super important; for example, if you are an outbound agent making hundreds of calls a day, getting rejected can be quite tough psychologically. You need to be OK with getting rejected. If you are a dedicated account manager and you are working on very high-level accounts, you might be working for seven months trying to close the deal and then all of a sudden it just goes south and you lose it.'

Kristen Gonzalez, VIP Brand Promoter, Thrive, notes what happens when you lack resilience:

> 'People come across problems and because they don't know how to solve them, they just throw in the towel and give up on themselves way too quickly where they're probably right on the brink of success and if they had just stuck it out a little bit longer, they'd be excelling.'

Motivation for resilience

Resilience can be learned over time and with experience, the right attitude and a tolerance towards risk.

Gertjan Rossing, Head of Delivery, CRM Partners, describes how his attitude towards risk and resilience changed as he moved from project management to sales:

> 'When you are a classic project manager, you focus on risks. As a sales guy, you need to encounter risks with elasticity and perseverance so you can grow your company. If you are aware of those risks and you manage them well, then you are in the perfect zone. In sales I learned to look at risks in a different way. Taking more risks, growing the group, growing the company by continuously stretching your limits. If you are not optimistic, you do not get the job done.'

Andrew Santos, CEO, Compass Group, shares his advice for ensuring resilience:

'I always tell people six letters: R-Y-B-L-A-B. Run Your Business Like A Business. That is always the lens we go back to in sales because it is so easy to go, "I don't feel like working." Well, that is irrelevant, you are running a business, so you have got to run it like a business, and get out there and go to work.'

KEY TAKEAWAY

A determined attitude and resilience are essential to bounce back from the inevitable disappointments in sales. If you don't have them, develop them quickly.

Lesson 5: You need curiosity and coachability

Business acumen and 'selling lamps' well

The need to acquire and retain information, both about sales and about your chosen industry, is essential in sales.

The trope of a typical salesperson selling 'lamps to a genie' (or similar) came up a few times in interviews, but Avi Wiesenberg, CRO and startup advisor, put an interesting twist on it:

'People say, "I can sell a lamp to a genie," without knowing anything about lamps or genies.

I think, if you want to sell lamps to genies, you have to become somewhat adept in understanding the needs of the genies and the nuances within lamps. Can you learn these things? Are you interested enough in lamps and genies? The number one thing I look for in a salesperson when I hire them is business acumen – sheer curiosity. Are you actually interested in what is going on in the world of business? Are you reading business pages?'

You need curiosity

Slim Earle of The Chemistry Group shares his thoughts on curiosity:

'The baseline characteristic we measure is the personal development capability. What we see in differentiating high-performing salespeople is a high level of curiosity – their willingness to learn and to challenge themselves. Great salespeople are often activist-learning types, so they learn by doing, not by theory. What we find is, regardless of the driver of that capability, people who are higher in personal development are better at other capabilities. It unlocks other capabilities, and it is a foundational differentiator when it comes to performance.'

You need coachability

Jamie Badar, CEO, V2R, says:

> 'I think the only thing is a willingness to learn, a willingness to invest and bravery to step out of the comfort zone. The personality trait is someone who needs to invest in themselves. I don't mean money, I mean time. The good results are always going to come from that level of discomfort. People who are willing to stay within their comfort zone, they will not get results.'

Kristen Gonzalez, VIP Brand Ambassador, Thrive, explains her key to success:

> 'Coachability – following in the footsteps of other people who have done it. I think sometimes you could try and do it your own way, but if people have already figured out a way that it works, why would you not just do what they do? It's just like in sports – someone has done it before.'

KEY TAKEAWAY

If you're curious and coachable, it will serve you well in sales.

Lesson 6: It's a challenge, so be a Challenger

Sales is a challenge

As Josef Dvorak, Country Manager, SBR Consulting, says:

> 'I would ask aspiring salespeople if they were ready for a challenge. Because sales equals challenge – a constant and never-ending challenge. I would really get bored being in a "normal" job. The challenge, even though it's one of the downsides, is also the upside for maniacs like me and for people who want to really succeed.'

To deal with a challenging career path, one of the most effective ways is to be a Challenger yourself. The idea of needing to be well-informed, not rely on personal relationships and occasionally being tough on prospects frequently came up in interviews.

Jon Begg, Head of Trade Marketing, RB, notes:

> 'If I look at how buying decisions are made, buyers now have a huge amount of data at their disposal – anything from a basic model through to proper artificial intelligence helping them to make that decision in a much more objective way. The traditional relationship and relationship-building is becoming a little less important. What's becoming more important is disruptive thinking, the ability to stand out a little bit and finding the insight that

really changes the frame of the reference. That requires a slightly different skillset; it requires somebody who wants to dig deep to understand what is going to be disruptive and what's going to get the attention of the buyer.'

The Challenger sales model

The Challenger sale model is based on the results of a seminal study of over 10,000 salespeople in a sales book titled *The Challenger Sale: How to take control of the customer conversation*.[7] The study focused on business-to-business (B2B) salespeople and identified three factors necessary for the modern salesperson to be successful:

1. Teaching prospects something new

2. Tailoring your presentations

3. Taking control of the sales process

Brett Goodyear, Head of Sales EMEA, Challenger Inc, explains:

> 'It's traditionally been said, "You've got to be gregarious. You've got to like people." In reality that's true, but don't like people too much. A lot of times they're going to say "no" and sometimes you've got to be tough with them if you're in a negotiation. That's where Challenger would say "relationship builders", or what we unofficially

---

7   B Adamson and M Dixon, *The Challenger Sale: How to take control of the customer conversation* (Portfolio Penguin, 2012)

term "people-pleasers", actually struggle the most in sales. If you're a people-pleaser you're in the wrong game because it's not about pleasing people. It's about driving value and getting people to make tough choices.

'If you're not a Challenger, it doesn't matter how good you are at technical sales. If you lack some of the other skills that are needed now as a professional seller – customer understanding, the ability to understand different communication styles, figuring out how a business ticks, finding moments to persuade and moments to rely on process, then you'll struggle.'

Challenger techniques can be learned

The good news is that Challenger techniques can be learned. Brett Goodyear went on to share an experience that demonstrates this:

'I honestly think that Challenger skills are completely teachable and I've seen them being taught to people. We once ran a pilot programme in Zambia and South Africa. The sellers were engineers, most of whom had been in sales less than a couple of years. I remember when I was working with our consulting team saying, "Can we get these guys to be Challengers?" They were very immature sellers, and we've had so many organisations say to us, "Challenger is too advanced for us. We need to get our basics right." Sure enough, we taught them and they closed deals. They used their technical knowledge and converted it into a business problem. We helped them build a teaching message and they were then able to scale that message across multiple customers. They actually preferred it because they said, "Hang on. What you're telling is I've got to tell a story that's about a technical problem that can cost them thousands and it's something that I can do twenty times over and over again? Fantastic." Challenging a customer with new knowledge is a teachable skill.'

KEY TAKEAWAY

The decline of the relationship-based sale was a common theme throughout my conversations and Challengers seem to be becoming more valuable over time. It should be noted that an exception to this is that in high-volume, tangible product sales, hard work and discipline (lessons 60 and 61) can work in the place of Challenger behaviour.

Lesson 7: Your suitability as a salesperson

Subjective personality testing

Peter Kiddle, MD, Business Transfer Agent, advises:

'If it is something you think you are going to be good at, if it is something you have spoken to lots of people about, got feedback from people you work with, talked with previous bosses about, discussed with the neighbour... Get feedback from everybody to see what they think about you in a potential sales role, then make a decision based on data.'

Trend towards self-diagnosis

Slim Earle of The Chemistry Group says:

'There is now an emerging trend of people self-diagnosing, and we have seen this in the world of recruitment. The selection process now is not just about me selling myself to you. It is about us collectively discovering whether this is a place where I can be brilliant, which is a completely different framing. If you are fairly new to the world of work, I think the more self-awareness and the more tools you have to reflect on what really drives you and really energises you, the more powerful you become in your job search.'

The quest for tests

In one of my earliest interviews, Charlie Kline, MD, Century Equity Partners, suggested that quantitative tests of ability were becoming more prominent in the workplace. He recalled a colleague telling him that everyone in their company takes a personality test and everyone knows the results of everyone else's test. It was the result of such a test that showed Charlie's colleague that selling was not a perfect fit for his personality. This sparked my interest in finding out more about sales aptitude tests.

Tests available

I interviewed leaders from both The Chemistry Group and Owiwi, as well as consultants who used third-party tests. A variety of tests to consider can be found here: www.exceptionalsalescareer.com/resources.

There are some in the profession who believe that, with or without tests, anyone can pursue a sales career. Stuart Lotherington, MD, SBR Consulting, says:

'If you look at analytical individuals or expressive individuals, I think both could be good at sales, and I say that having trained, managed and recruited 2,500 students before I started my fourteen-year career in consulting. I think I can honestly say anyone can do it.'

KEY TAKEAWAY

Sales might be easier for some personality types than others but it is ultimately how comfortable you are with the sales process that should determine your choice to pursue this career path.

2
Lessons In The Downside Of Sales

'I'd say choose the challenges you want, not the good bits that you want. Choose which difficulties you can put up with. For sales, it's the pressure, the low lows, the travel, the uncomfortable conversations. These are all things that you will do because you're excited about the outcome. If you're choosing sales based on only the good bits, I see a lot of people not having a good time.'
— Howard Paine, Regional Sales Manager, Zscaler

Lesson 8: Sales has a stigma

Salespeople are not always respected

Unfortunately, sales does have a stigma attached and is generally viewed with suspicion, sometimes to the extent that even salespeople themselves are embarrassed to admit what they do as a career. Anne-Marie

Lee, Senior Manager, Aviva, held strong views about salespeople before her current role:

> 'I thought they were really scumbags because some of them have very big egos and they really do the hard sell. It's all about how great they are, how successful they are and insurance agents trying to sell me the accolades of the rich and famous clients that they had which I really didn't care about. I didn't think they were very ethical.'

Zander Fryer, CEO, High Impact Coaching, feels that the trend has changed:

> 'This world is done with greasy, grimy, manipulative, pushy, pressurised sales. It's done with it. It's been three or four decades' worth of sleazy, greasy stuff and all these people who are pushing snake oil or negative messages made a bunch of money and swindled grandma out of her hard-earned cash. The old, pushy, manipulative sales tactics are on the way out. This world is too smart… They want real. They want trustworthy. Sales itself isn't a good or a bad thing. It's just a tool and it can be used and leveraged for good or bad. But when you're a good person leveraging sales, you actually just get to spread good. It's a tool for influence.'

There are no degrees for sales

There are no degrees for sales careers. Sales isn't taught in schools either, and even the teaching of sales in universities is at an early stage.

Avi Wiesenberg, CRO and startup advisor, says:

'I did a business degree, and it was just not there. There was no "Sales 101". I think maybe universities have started doing that now in the business degrees and the MBAs, but sales was just not respected as a profession or as any type of science. Today you have got that ability to really crunch the numbers and the data and there is a huge amount of scientific research being done into what we have always felt is true.'

Dimitry Toukhcher, CEO, LGFG Fashion House, agrees:

'There is no medical degree to get into sales. If I go to a doctor's office and he treats me, I don't ask the doctor about his credentials. I just believe that doctors are there because they are allowed to be. After all, they have gone through a massive amount of training to ensure that they should be treating me. That doesn't happen with salespeople, so there's less trust initially.'

KEY TAKEAWAY

In the words of the Peter Parker Principle: 'With great power comes great responsibility.'[8] You will need to earn your reputation as a salesperson.

Lesson 9: There'll be some internal resistance and resentment

Sales has a reputation

In almost every organisation that I've been a part of – consumer goods, media or advisory services – non-sales functions have had a problem with sales, be it regarding relative standards of pay, or how little we seem to typically work. Hans Keijmel, Strategic Account Director, Bloomreach, agrees:

> 'Outside of sales everyone always thinks that we do nothing in sales. They think that we are always on the beach, that we drive really cool cars, that we are always flying. Basically, that we are working from ten to three, but they forget the pressure that we are under. When you become better under pressure, sales is a really good job. Until then, it is like a marathon but you have to run at sprint speed.'

---

8   M Pigliucci, 'The Peter Parker principle' (Medium, 3 August 2020), https://massimopigliucci.medium.com/the-peter-parker-principle-9f3f33799904, accessed 16 November 2020

Gertjan Rossing, Head of Delivery, CRM Partners, has seen both sides:

'I was a project manager in the past, and others sold solutions and projects for me. I thought to myself, how is it possible that the salespeople sell stuff and all I seem to do is fix their mistakes? I thought I'd move to the other side and with my experience, I could do it better. I then learned that sales is a craft. It is something you need to learn, you need to improve and that it is a real job. That was my conclusion: from the other side it might look easy, but it is not easy. It is a real job.'

Sales can be actively disliked

Tomas Mesteller, Chief Commercial Officer (CCO), Orbit, commissioned some research into this area:

'One thing that we learned from the programme is that salespeople are generally perceived negatively in our industry. The thoughts and feelings usually aren't positive when you say "salesperson". Many people, like my colleagues or consultants, when I ask them to help us with sales, they expect something deviant or something that is outside of their comfort zone.'

Some may resent your earnings

And then there's the money. Avi Wiesenberg, CRO and startup advisor, says:

'There is a huge misperception within some organisations from non-salespeople. They may say, "Hey, you're getting paid on this deal, give me a bit of your commission because I helped out on it as well," to which I'd reply, "Hey, that's my salary. It just happens to be that my salary is heavily geared towards performance as opposed to yours, and you get paid whether you deliver or not."'

KEY TAKEAWAY

Colleagues in other areas of the business may dislike you for being in sales and may wrongly perceive your role or efforts.

Lesson 10: Targets create constant pressure

No hiding in sales

When I asked my interviewees, 'What is the worst thing about being in sales?' some form of pressure or performance-based scrutiny was mentioned over 60% of the time. You need to be able to handle pressure.

Hans Keijmel, Strategic Account Director, Bloomreach, puts it bluntly:

> 'If you do not like the pressure of sales, just quit. Just start immediately in another job because when you cannot work with the pressure that is already on your shoulders from day one, you will never be able to do it.'

Raf Tristao, Head of Strategic Accounts, DB Insights, says:

> 'If you have monthly or quarterly targets, what you did last month on day one of the next month doesn't matter; it's out the window, you need to do it again. When you're doing well, it is excellent – you get rewarded and you get praised. When you're not doing well, look at it like gambling. When you're up, you're up and when you're down, it doesn't feel good. It's what you do with that feeling of failure that kind of decides whether or not you're going to be a great salesperson or not.'

Pressure can undermine you

Dimitry Toukhcher, CEO, LGFG Fashion House, says:

> 'Sales is very character-revealing; it's sometimes hard to quickly figure out a person's character traits and ability to be persistent. It can undermine your self-belief. It can even change your political views on things because you realise how much

of success is self-determined, which I am aware is really not a popular opinion in today's world. Confronting that reality and having to repeatedly persevere when you don't want to can be pretty challenging.'

Ronald Sluiter, Global Client Director, Gartner, is just as candid:

'To be transparent, I always think, "What am I doing in sales? Why am I doing this? Why am I loving this?" Because it is a hard job, especially when you've done it for a while and you are getting older. Keeping the flow, keeping that energy and keeping yourself fit so you can recover quickly becomes harder. The constant switch from "hero to zero" and back in a few months becomes harder, and then you are all over the place. Yes, it is the pressure that is the hardest thing.'

KEY TAKEAWAY

If you can handle the intensity and pressure of targets; with a combination of resilience, hard work and sales talk, you'll be well suited to sales.

Lesson 11: You're going to be 'always on'

Starting off is tough, and you'll need to work hard

One of the perceived benefits of a sales career is that you work a limited schedule – that you can only reach out during hours when your clients are online. Most of the salespeople I interviewed did not exhibit this behaviour at all.

Stuart Lotherington, MD, SBR Consulting, is keen to debunk this myth:

> 'The reason why people outside of sales do not really get this right is that you are not doing nine-to-five in sales. You do not just turn up and then go, "Right, I am going to dial." Of course, some organisations do that, but I think the successful salespeople are the ones who look to get slight edges, which means you might be working in the evenings or you might be doing the early morning calls or whatever, and that effort often goes unseen. For example, networking in the evenings if you are in business development. It is all out of your own personal calendar, and therefore you need to be rewarded for that effort.'

Hugo Barclay, Owner, ArtThou, agrees:

> 'If I was an accountant, then once I finish my balance sheet for the quarter it's done. I can switch my computer off by six, I can go home. This doesn't

happen when you are doing a sales job. It feels hard to switch off when you can always be doing more. There is always that thought in the back of your mind later, "Who else is working harder?"'

No true holidays

Ultimately, the reason that top performers constantly work so hard is to ensure their pipeline of business is strong (lesson 60).

Radoslav Ivanov, International Sales Executive, Historical Park Bulgaria, says:

> 'Honestly, the worst thing is to stop being on a roll. I do not know if you have ever jumped in a pool when you were a kid and you were looking at the water thinking, "Oh my God. I cannot believe it. I am going to drown." You get all those shaky feelings, those butterflies in your belly. But when you jump once you are like, "Oh, I think I can do that twice." Then you go again and you still have those butterflies. But then when you jump after fifteen times, you think, "Why did I even have those butterfly feelings?" It's like that in sales. Never stop selling.'

It was interesting listening to John Schlegel, CEO, Stonebridge Search, talk about his holiday plans:

> 'I tell myself, "I'm actually doing well financially. I have flexibility. I should just take advantage of that and go get a little break." I almost have a clock

in my head set for every eight to ten weeks. I take a little vacation – in most cases, it's three days. I mean it's two or three days. In fact, I take my laptop with me. I still work a little bit in the mornings.'

KEY TAKEAWAY

The best salespeople I interviewed are terrible at switching off from their jobs because they love the process, the results, or both. I have met salespeople who do work typical schedules, and that's fine – but their results reflect that.

Lesson 12: There will be conflict, and people will say 'no'

Sales includes conflict

I distinctly remember my first 'no' and it stung. I was aged eight and selling raffle tickets in my dad's office. It was fertile ground – the office workers were generally affluent, the raffle tickets relatively inexpensive, and it definitely helped that I was the boss's son. I had come in the top ten of my school's raffle ticket sales the year before and was determined to come first this year.

Everyone but one lady bought. She quickly ushered me out, citing my ineffective raffle ticket from the year before as a reason for not buying. I was quite put out and complained to my dad. He said, 'People have to be able to say "no". Are you going to let it put you off selling the most raffle tickets?' I didn't. I sold the most. I even had another go at selling to the same lady, though in retrospect I'm glad that she said 'no' again.

Howard Paine, Regional Sales Manager, Zscaler, puts his recommendation concisely:

> 'I think if you're not comfortable sitting in an uncomfortable conversation and holding your own, or if your aim is to avoid that kind of conflict, then I'd probably say going into sales might not be your thing.'

Charlie Kline, MD, Century Equity Partners, adds:

> 'I think you have to be good at reading people, which not all people are. Having read them, you have to be able to both put them at ease and put them at unease at your discretion. You challenge them. Perhaps point out things they aren't aware of that puts them ill at ease but in the end, you're trying to bring them back around to your point of view.'

Sales includes rejection

Eric Hirschberg, CEO, Echo Finance, says:

'The main thing is how you process "no", because you're in the process of building relationships. You're going to get a lot of rejection, and it's how you embrace rejection and what you do with it that defines whether you're going to be good at it or not. People who internalise and personalise rejection tend to not do well in sales because they're too busy with their own egos – "It's about me, it's not about the other person."'

Zander Fryer, CEO, High Impact Coaching, has an optimistic view of rejection:

'Sales is hard. You are a professional rejection artist. You're a professional failure, you hear "no" all the time. You're constantly failing. You're constantly getting out of your comfort zone. If you want sales to be easy, you're in the wrong industry. It's not easy but it's worth it. You can have a much bigger impact than you can anywhere else.'

How to handle it

Stuart Lotherington, MD, SBR Consulting, gives this advice:

'The biggest challenge is the mental toughness that you need in sales. A lot of us will reach out to a few friends, and if a friend does not call us back after dropping them a couple of texts, we deem that as rejection and we consider what we've done to them. They are probably just busy people. That is the case in most of our environments. If you start taking that personally or if you do not form mental strategies on how to overcome that kind of rejection, you're in trouble.'

KEY TAKEAWAY

If you can learn to not take rejection personally and not let it prevent you from taking the necessary actions, you'll be in good stead. If not, you should seriously consider not doing sales.

Lesson 13: You'll never get it exactly right

You just need to take action

Sales is not for perfectionists, and sometimes issues arise that can never be fully resolved. Sometimes you just need to try and do your best to learn (see lesson 5), especially in younger businesses. Dimitry Toukhcher, CEO, LGFG Fashion House, says this to aspiring salespeople: 'Get ready to get your ass kicked. Take it like a champion.'

Katrin Kiviselg, Partner, The NorthStar Consulting Group, works with a lot of startups:

'The first salesperson in any startup should not be a "thinker" type of person, if you know what

I mean. They should be a "doer". Sometimes they just need to go out and find a way.'

Lee McCroskey, speaker, trainer and coach, Southwestern Speakers, reflects on why issues may arise when you work to get it exactly right:

> 'I always thought that working a tough sales job was good for perfectionists because there were so many variables in the equation. It is like a multi-variable calculus equation and you can get a couple of those equations right, and then miss some of them. For perfectionists, who like to have everything in place, every jot and tittle just so; it does not work.'

You need patience

Teresa Sproul, Sales Leader, Tom James, gives this advice:

> 'Be very patient. Anything that you will get big results from is going to take a lot of work and it's going to take a lot of effort, and you might not always see results immediately. You always have to be planting seeds, and you don't know if they're going to grow tomorrow or in a year. I feel like with training new partners now, a lot of them want results quickly, and it's not always like that.'

KEY TAKEAWAY

Not all sales calls will go to plan and you won't always be right, but if you can accept that, then the challenge of sales might be for you.

Lesson 14: The nature of sales is changing

Simple sales jobs may be automated as customers move online

There is a growing awareness within the industry that many of the 'traditional product' salespeople may no longer be needed in an increasing era of online purchases and automation.

Steve Goknel, CEO, Your Edge, says:

'In terms of retail, I think it's dead. E-commerce has been chipping away and that's been making it harder for the last ten years and I have been aware of that. I have come to the realisation that it's flogging a dead horse, and e-commerce has become ten times easier. So, that's why I switched my business direction.'

Sugato Deb, Head of Sales Enablement, National Instruments, drives home the issue for the modern product salesperson:

'It is easy to go to a customer and say, "My product does XYZ." It disregards the situation that the customer holds most of the knowledge. They understand the problem, and it is up to the salesperson to show how they can add value. The role of the collaborator in bringing people together, whether it is inside your organisation or helping the customer's organisation, will be increasingly valued. These softer skills will be a big part of the next generation. The product and features demos are now becoming more readily available to customers on websites. They'll go to our website and look at our customer stories, trying to get an agnostic view.'

More decision-makers and longer processes

The other major B2B issue is an increase in the purchasing complexity for organisations. As Brett Goodyear, Head of Sales EMEA, Challenger Inc, says:

'The increase in the number of stakeholders, more decisions going to a non-decision, more procurement people coming into the mix, more requests to customise offerings but not necessarily recognising the value of those customised offerings, and more price-based decisions are all modern issues. There are more "status quo" decisions – "I'll just take what I've got now. The cost for me and the personal risk of making a change is far greater than the value that you're offering me because I've got to go and convince these other ten people, many of whom probably don't even sit in the same department as me, never mind the same country or same part of the business."'

Tomas Mesteller, Chief Commercial Officer, Orbit, understands the struggle:

'It's really energy-draining when you have delivered a good presentation, you've found all the needs, you see the buy-in on the other side, and their future user is enthusiastic about it, but afterwards you know what lies ahead of you is three to four months of procurement and decision-making. There'll be investment committees, continual workshops, more presentations – it happens all the time.'

Powerful customers

Sugato Deb, Head of Sales Enablement, National Instruments, says:

'I think the biggest single piece of research was one by Gartner, that customers are 57% of their way through a purchase before they have contact with the seller. This wasn't aligned with my thinking at the time; that sales are essentially a reactive force to the customer figuring out what they want. But it also opened up the question regarding what was happening during that 57%, and how participation in that period can be much more effective, and it changed a lot of mindsets including the approach of some multi-national companies.'

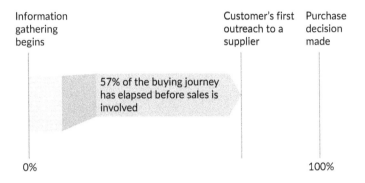

| Information gathering begins | | Customer's first outreach to a supplier | Purchase decision made |

57% of the buying journey has elapsed before sales is involved

0%   100%

The sales journey

KEY TAKEAWAY

To succeed in today's complex sales environment you need to present brilliantly when you get an opportunity (lesson 62), prepare excellently (lesson 95), own your industry (lesson 94) and collaborate well with marketing (lesson 46).

3
Lessons In What's Great About Sales

'There's a statistic that if you like your job 30% or more, you should probably stay where you are; most people are around 30% content with their jobs. I think the most successful salespeople move that stat way up. I've met and trained and worked with salespeople that have been 90% or 95% satisfied with their career in terms of making a difference in helping others.'

— Theo Davies, Head of Cloud Sales Enablement JAPAC, Google

Lesson 15: Freedom and flexibility

Freedom

The biggest single answer to 'What's great about sales?', when I asked the question to over 100 interviewees, was freedom and/or flexibility.

Ron Alford, Senior Partner, SBR Consulting, explains:

> 'I love how you can make your choice. You can set your goals, you can choose to ebb and flow. You know, "OK, this next season, I'm going to focus a little bit more on my family, and I'm going to maintain my production," or, "This next few months, man, I'm going to buckle down. I'm going to get permission from my family to go deeper here and take this to another level." You have that freedom.'

Katrin Kiviselg, Partner, NorthStar Consulting, agrees:

> 'Number one is freedom – when somebody cracks how a successful sale is done, they will also understand that the whole world is now open to them. By the whole world, I really mean the whole world. Not only can you choose a career on your terms but you can also move to any country at any point in time. You can find a job anywhere.'

Flexibility

Greg James, financial advisor at a major US bank, says:

> 'My daughter, who is also an employee here, used to be a trouble-shooter for Starbucks, and that gave her perspective. She had no control over time. She had to work every holiday, every Christmas, every Thanksgiving. Now she comes in, she works very hard, as I do, but if either of us wants to go to her

daughter's school for a performance, we can. I'm on five different non-profit boards. Anything we want to do, as long as we're working hard, we have complete time freedom, and we can structure our lives any way we want to.'

Rusty Branch, President, Compass Law, says:

'I have complete control of my schedule. I work with attorneys who will typically work eighty to a hundred hours a week and I find that, yes, they make a lot of money, but their satisfaction in life may not be up to par. I take a lot of value in the fact that I've got flexible work hours; that I can spend a lot of time with my family.'

How to get there

You don't always get freedom and flexibility immediately. In my first complex sales job with Debtwire, I was required to be at my desk from 8:30am to 6pm. You can typically earn increased flexibility by building a gradual combination of trust and credibility.

Avi Wiesenberg, CRO and startup advisor, says:

'One of the best pieces of advice I was given was from one of my ex-Oracle colleagues. I was a young, cocky Jewish sales guy at Oracle. He said, "This is the same as your dad's *shmatte* (fabric) business. The nice side is we are giving you a base salary, and we are giving you a phone, an office and a laptop. Those are your accounts. Go and make yourself some money, and run it like a franchise."'

KEY TAKEAWAY

Once you achieve a sales position reflecting your competence and performance, the freedom and flexibility is amazing.

Lesson 16: Enjoying personal interaction with people

People skills can't be automated

As discussed in lesson 2, not every salesperson needs to be a people person. However, you inevitably need to interact with people in sales, so you will certainly have a competitive advantage if you enjoy doing so.

Brad Revell, Senior Director, Infor, says:

'If you can work with people in a better way, understand what they're trying to get across with their words and their body language, and many other different indicators, then absolutely you have an advantage. There's a lot of automation going on now in the era we're in, a lot of the mundane tasks are going to be automated. What's going to be left is the bits where you're working with people. I believe you'd have a competitive advantage if you know how to deal with people better, understanding their needs and values and aligning yourself and your message to that.'

Avi Wiesenberg, CRO and startup advisor, agrees:

'In the product-driven, marketing-driven world, the salesperson is just the friction. However, I think there are always those people that will want to deal with the person. I also do not believe that you are going to go to a high-end restaurant for an experience and order through a kiosk. You know the difference when you have a good waiter. They just ask you two or three questions: "What brings you here this evening?" "Oh, we're having our anniversary." "Well, let me recommend this special bottle of wine…"'

Enjoyment of problem-solving for people is key

Theo Davies, Head of Cloud Sales Enablement JAPAC, Google, says:

'You would think that if you focus on your commission and you focus on your results, that you would perform at the highest level, when in fact you can't out-give your client. If you forget about yourself and focus purely on helping other people, serving other people, solving other people's problems, you ultimately win yourself as well, and you get paid for solving those problems.'

Greg James, financial advisor at a major US bank, epitomises how much some interviewees genuinely enjoy other people:

> 'With one of the boards I'm on, I served on the search committee for a new executive director. We found a great person, but afterwards they told me I was not of much use in the selection process. I asked, "Why was I useless?" After all, I was chairman of the board! "You're useless because you liked everybody." It's true – I like everybody, and I like everything that's going on. In good markets, that's fun, the clients are happy. In bad markets, you can find better bargains, and you're competing with fewer people, so I can handle any of it.'

KEY TAKEAWAY

If you enjoy people – whether it is working with them, understanding them or serving them – you'll have a lot of fun and a promising career in sales.

Lesson 17: You can choose to serve

Helping people

Related to enjoying and benefiting from interacting with people is the true passion to serve, which manifested in some of our more passionate interviewees.

Mark Cooper, Owner, Cooper and Lansbury Associates, says,

> 'Occasionally, I will spend two or three hours with someone, and it's not very often, but they will turn around say, "Oh my God. That was enlightening. I wish I'd known that five, ten, fifteen years ago." That is the absolute zenith of what I could want out of this – helping people be better at what they do. I have a mantra: "I can't make you smarter, but I can make you better." You can't make people more intelligent or approach things with a higher IQ than they already have, but you can make people better at what they do.'

Greg James, financial advisor, sees selling as a service:

> 'I have a friend who's a retired orthopaedic surgeon, and when people come to him and say that they are motorcycle riders, he doesn't try to talk them out of riding motorcycles. He will just say, "I think you should continue that, because our transplant doctors here are very much in favour of that." If you care about people, you sell them on something.'

Service is beneficial

According to some interviewees, service is the modern key to sales success. Zander Fryer, CEO, High Impact Coaching, says:

'People can smell "commission breath" over the phone. The most important skill, which is going to be different from what most people would probably say, is having the right intention. That intention is to actually help the other person that you are intending on selling something to. If you're in it to help people and you're not afraid to ask for money, you will become wildly successful.'

Andrew Santos, CEO, Compass Group, says:

'The most fulfilling is the opportunity to serve people, not just on a product level where you sell something that you really believe in and you know can help folks, but more on a leadership level. When you can help somebody learn something they do not know at the time and develop into a person with different skills, to achieve things that they have been encouraged to do outside their comfort zone and dream about.'

True galvanisation

Ron Alford, Senior Partner, SBR Consulting, reflects on the galvanisation of success:

'When you see others succeed, and they're part of your team, then there's this mutual celebration. It's just such that I get goosebumps talking about it. It's such fun. To me, it's just like you see the ripple effect. If they're growing, their families are impacted and it just spreads. And so that's the team piece, it's just so much more impactful and meaningful.'

JT Olson, CEO, Both Hands Foundation, literally sells service, as the lead fundraiser for a charity which supports both widows and orphans:

'For me, it is about our families saying, "We're going to serve a widow. In the process, we're going to fund an adoption, and there's about twenty or thirty people who are going to give their life away for a day fixing up a widow's house. They're going to walk away fulfilled. They're going to feel like they have made a difference in this widow's life and they are helping to bring an orphan home." It doesn't get any better than that. I think my job's easy. It's irresistible.'

KEY TAKEAWAY

Like each of these phenomenal salespeople, you can find true galvanisation by choosing what you sell (lesson 32) and actively serving the people that you sell to.

Lesson 18: You can quantify your impact

Sales is quantifiable

The measurability of sales, and the certainty of success if you follow the process (lesson 64) and hit your top-line numbers (lesson 60) is highly attractive to some salespeople.

Carolin Berger, Regional Sales Director, Outpost24, talks about her move into the field:

> 'In sales, I think if you do a good job, if you treat your customers well, if you listen to them well, you have that direct feedback of happy customers and successful sales. That is what I find most rewarding – that there is instant feedback, not a long, delayed process after months and months before someone finally says, "Oh, that is a nice project that you implemented. Thank you for that." Sometimes, in other positions, it is hard to measure if someone is doing a good job or not. People can hide and be vague about their contribution to a team effort. However, in sales, it is very transparent. Either you do a good job, or you do not.'

Dimitry Toukhcher, CEO, LGFG Fashion House, agrees:

> 'I like the fact that my results are objective. I really wanted fairness, and that is an important principle of mine. Sales is very fair because sales are an objective measure of one's performance. There cannot

be some 360-degree employee review with KPIs [key performance indicators] and objectives and subjective tendencies or how much I like someone. It allows you to just look at the numbers; it is all there, and the results will never lie.'

Numbers make goal setting easier

Quantification helps with setting your goals (lesson 89) as well. Rick Halbrooks, Vice President of Sales, McLeod Software, says:

'A lot of folks don't know their goals in their jobs. Somebody who's a programmer – they know that their goal is to get finished with a certain program but is the time clearly defined? How you know whether it's a great job or a good job? I don't know how you do all those things, which is why I'm in sales. I like the idea of having clearly defined, objective goals.'

Larger impact on business and economy

Aside from being quantifiable for the individual, sales can also have a quantifiable impact on a business or the wider economy. Richard Humphreys, former CEO, Saatchi & Saatchi, says:

'Sales is very important – new business is the prime objective to maintain morale and to improve the finances, and therefore, I always invested heavily in the new business departments.'

Robin Mukherjee, MD, 2Circles Consulting, feels that sales are the primary economic driver:

> 'Absolutely – no sales, no business, no jobs, no cash and no cash flow. Sales is the king for any business to get on its feet, to survive and to thrive. Businesses can burn through a lot of cash. However, if they can raise their top-line, then that allows them the room to operate when they have a good sales function.'

KEY TAKEAWAY

If you like growth, numbers and knowing your impact, then sales is a good option for you.

Lesson 19: You will develop and grow

Continuous learning is required

Given the potential diversity of experience in the sales field and the modernisation of sales (lesson 14), learning to develop and grow is a great thing for salespeople – and it's not optional. Zander Fryer, CEO, High Impact Coaching, says, 'There's a lot of different roles out there. It allows a lot of people to just settle into a comfort zone, settle into mediocrity, but sales just isn't one of them.'

Jamie Badar, CEO, V2R Coaching, says:

'I think it's a privilege to be able to gain insights from experienced business operators, experts, entrepreneurs – to understand what their challenges are, how they work and what their aspirations are. To be able to get insight into the nuances of their businesses, their challenges, their aspirations, and to be able to know that my offering is able to contribute to their success is rewarding. The higher you go in terms of the food chain – you could be dealing with some country-level critical projects, supply of energy to a country, for example – the more exhilarating the sales process.'

The learning is not just in sales

John Willis, Director, 2Circles Communications, shares what he considers to be the most fulfilling thing about sales:

'Personal growth, in short. The various forms of sales, sales management, and sales leadership that I've been involved in. Every single lesson that you learn in the field of selling – whether you're selling solutions, whether you're selling directly to end users, whether you're selling to businesses or you're selling your vision to colleagues, teammates and employees – all of these things can apply directly into every other part of everyday life. Everything you learn in your day-to-day business can be directly applied to your private life, your sports life, your social life, and how you deal with challenges. There is no other role within industries that offers that richness of experience.'

The habit of setting life goals often extends beyond the field of the profession. Interestingly, Jason Dial, Chairman, LGFG Fashion House, says, 'Usually, when I start working with single salespeople after they start setting and achieving goals, suddenly they are married.'

Theresa Sproul, Sales Leader, Tom James, explains how the sales environment often serves to strengthen relationships:

> 'The fact that it's so hard – a lot of times this creates more of like a family environment. Everyone's there to support each other, help, and people care about each other's wellbeing. At the end of the day, I am 100% different in so many good ways because of the challenges, and I met my husband through selling. All of my friends are people that I work with or people that I've worked with in the past between Southwestern and Tom James. My whole life would be different if I hadn't gone into this career.'

KEY TAKEAWAY

There you have it: work in sales and you'll get married. On a more serious note, though, you will experience growth and increased discipline through sales (lesson 63) – with the advantage that this will carry over into your personal life.

Lesson 20: Your experiences will be diverse

You can work in various industries

No industry is the same and sales skills are highly transferrable, which generally allows the freedom and flexibility (lesson 15) you can get from sales. Connie Smith, Consultant, Whitten & Roy Partnership, says:

> 'I think what's exciting about sales is that it's not restricted to any industry or sector. What I love is that I have the ability to work in education and property and technology and then eventually I've managed to find my niche, which is within development, so working with social enterprises and organisations in Africa. Regardless of whether you're working in America, the UK, or Africa, it's a really transferable skill and so I've been able to travel with my work.'

Venetia Paske, Principal Consultant, SBR Consulting, suggests actively looking for opportunities that offer diversity:

> 'I would always advise looking for breadth, and an organisation which can offer you a breadth of

different opportunities within that; whether that's different verticals within that business or different businesses within the group or different country offices, if there is a passion for travelling on the international side.'

Your days are diverse

Aside from the diversity of role, industry and location, even individual days are diverse in sales. Tomas Mesteller, CCO, Orbit, says:

'Every day brings something new and even though you plan – my day starts with some sort of a scheduled agenda in preparing what's ahead of me for today – in reality, the schedule is rarely kept. Something happens, and you need to adapt. The agenda is re-evaluated for either something positive or negative. The lack of routine is something I like.'

Ollie Venn, Operations Director, Foxtons, agrees:

'You're constantly being challenged every day. We have the best salespeople in the world, we have the best product in the world to sell, but there won't be the same scenario twice over. Every single day you should theoretically be presented with either a different scenario or with the same scenario but different people, circumstances or whatever the case may be. That's a lot of fun.'

Your challenges and skills are diverse

Ryan Dowd, Business Development Manager, COMATCH, says:

> 'The best thing about being in sales is that I have the opportunity to learn something new every day. The diversity of the clients that I work with is amazing, and the diversity of the problems that they need to solve. Nobody expects a salesperson to be the expert; there is a product guy for that. One of my talents is being able to get up to speed quickly on a new subject – I can get to an intelligent and conversational level with the topic very quickly.'

There is some science behind sales skills being transferrable. As Ilias Vartholomaios, CEO, Owiwi, says: 'There is to a very large degree a strong overlap – about 60% to 70% – in what skills are thought to be necessary across all regions for salespeople.'

KEY TAKEAWAY

If diversity is what you desire, then sales has it all: diversity of industry, daily routine and challenges.

Lesson 21: You can advance quickly and become a CEO

Reasons you can advance quickly

Sales does not have a defined career path, and that can be a good thing if your aim is to advance fast and become a CEO, especially early in life.

Connie Smith, Consultant, Whitten & Roy Partnership, says:

> 'Having worked with thousands of people in sales, I find that when they take personality tests, typically the most successful tend to be those that want to be leaders; they've got to be confident and quite independent.'

Nazma Qurban, CRO, Cognism, says:

> 'If you go into any other career, usually, you are not really in control of what your progression will look like. Most of the time, you will go into a graduate or intern role. You are there for two years. Then you get to progress into another role, and you are there for five years. There is not as much control as you can gain from being in sales if you are a high performer. You would expect to be promoted a lot more quickly because you actually have the results to prove that you have the ability and capability to step up.'

Avi Wiesenberg, CRO and startup advisor, tells the story of successfully getting into an unlikely company:

> 'I failed my entry physics exam. The interviewer was like, "Well, everyone in the company has got a PhD in physics. I do not think you can be involved in helping our service." I was like, "Mate, I am not going to do the technical side of the sale. Someone else has to do that. There is a whole other element of the sale that you guys do not understand, which is the human side of the sale. The commercial side of the sale is completely different."'

Companies need sales, and you won't necessarily need qualifications to get your foot in the door (lessons 53–58).

Switching jobs

Likewise, you can accelerate your career by switching companies, or roles within a company. Phil Low, Growth Lead, Revolut, found moving earned him a quick promotion:

> 'Moving to Revolut, a high-growth company where that particular business unit was far less mature, was appealing. I didn't join Revolut to be a sales lead and to run the sales team, but that's how the cards fell.'

Lauri Kinkar, CEO, Messente Communications, explains why salespeople advance so fast:

> 'You have a very good understanding of the product. You have a very good understanding of the value of competition and the customer profile, which means that sales is the ultimate springboard for any other job in that company. I have seen a lot of salespeople ending up as head of operations and advancing to the highest management levels.'

Become the CEO

If you want to be a CEO, be that in a big or small company, sales is a viable route to get there. Brett Goodyear, Head of Sales EMEA, Challenger Inc, says:

> 'If you look at more and more CEO roles now, more and more of these guys are coming from sales. Ten to twenty years ago they were coming from marketing. Thirty to forty years ago they came from finance or accounting or engineering. I think of the most aggressive new companies – these guys are salespeople.'

Ronald Suiter, Global Client Director, Gartner, says:

> 'There was a study of Fortune 500 CEOs recently about how the majority now have sales backgrounds. It was about 70%, because sales is about connecting people. It is understanding people and

asking the right questions instead of having all the answers.'

KEY TAKEAWAY

Whether you have modest ambitions of continued career advancement or eyes for the top, sales as a career is a good option.

Lesson 22: You can make serious money

There's no shame in wanting remuneration

There wasn't a single person in the series of 105 interviews who didn't touch on money in some shape or form, with almost universally positive feedback on how much a salesperson can earn.

Simon Ruddick, Chairman, Albourne Partners, puts it eloquently:

> 'My dearly beloved father was subprime before it was fashionable and went bust twice in my childhood. That gave me a deep and lasting respect for solvency. I've been very committed to the pursuit of solvency. A colleague of mine once referred to his life goal as to be "fabulously solvent" and I've adopted that as my own.'

Peter Kiddle, Chairman, Business Transfer Agent, will only employ those motivated in that way:

'I would always look for somebody that is hungry for money. I have never employed a salesperson on a capped income. I have never employed somebody as a salesperson where they are not hungry. It is important to me because it always drove me; you cannot just sit back and rely on your base salary. Although interestingly, it only works for a period of years. After that, you become so used to having a good income because the bonus and commissions that you are earning are always good, because you know you are going to do well anyway, that your motivation becomes achievement instead.'

Make it variable

The way to maximise your earnings in sales is to accept a greater amount of 'risk' and variability. I put 'risk' in quotation marks because, in my experience and many of the interviewees, the risk you take in variable earnings is hugely outweighed by the potentially massive rewards.

Mike Turner, MD, YouBecome, supports bonuses and commissions:

'The secret to motivate salespeople is to give them a massive bonus opportunity or commission opportunity. Sometimes salespeople don't like that, which is weird, I think. Absolutely bizarrely, some of these guys who are great salespeople would prefer to have a big old fat basic salary. Whereas you'd think the top sales guys would just love to have a huge accelerator and bonus structure.'

Scott Roy, CEO, Whitten & Roy Consultancy, says:

'I would say, really get to grips with variable pay and embrace it. If you're going to get into sales, get into something where you're going to get paid well, which means, you're going to take some risk on yourself that the lower the base salary the greater the opportunity there is. So therefore, you should be paid more for taking on this risk.'

KEY TAKEAWAY

Sales is definitely high on the risk and reward spectrum, but the combination of many sales potentially being secure through a combination of residual sales (lesson 34) and security in the maths of sales (lesson 60) means that much of your variable income should be secure.

4
Lessons In Sales Considerations

'What I find more fulfilling is seeing younger sellers come into the profession and seeing it becoming professionalised. You realise that actually there's a lot of process involved, there's a lot of science behind it now; that it is actually an art and a science. It's not all about salespeople wanting to run around earning as much commission as possible. There are people that genuinely believe in sales as a career and they are becoming sales leaders.'

— Brett Goodyear, Head of Sales Europe EMEA, Challenger Inc

Lesson 23: How to get started in sales

Assessment

You need to put some thought into your start in sales, in retrospect something I wish I had done. I jumped into the largest sales organisation that existed, Procter & Gamble (P&G), which ended up being a marketing- and product-led organisation, at least at the time.

Sam Lewis, Partner, Albourne Partners, says:

'This is the advice I give to people who are looking for jobs. Get a big piece of A3 and think of everything you know, everything you like, everything you don't like – put it down there. It's like one of those CGI-type images that you'll look at cross-eyed for long enough until all of a sudden you see a colour picture of dancing horses. Do you like big firms? Do you like smaller firms? There are plenty of considerations.'

There are also different skills and interests needed for different sales career paths. Eric Hirschberg, CEO, Echo Finance, agrees:

'If you're advising people who really want to go into sales, I think they have to do their own strength inventories and then figure out what kind of sales people they're going to be. They have to realise the shortcomings of whatever they're going to do. My method of building relationships and taking "noes" easily is not very good for car sales.'

Plan your career

Plenty of interviewees (almost 40% in fact) said that their biggest regret was less long-term career planning early on. Jamie Badar, CEO, V2R Coaching, says:

'You always get a lot of turnover with salespeople. They get sold into a job by recruitment consultants and it's very easy to be sold and also to move on if they're not happy in their current role. I've seen sales people just fall into an industry without the deliberation or time taken to discover where they would be most productive.'

Theresa Sproul, Sales Leader, Tom James, makes a suggestion:

'I would recommend taking a breath and having more of a long-term vision. Not just being in the moment, knowing what I'm working for. Having a clear idea of what I wanted in the future would probably be the biggest thing.'

Jump in and be agile

One thing you mustn't do is to overthink and never jump in. Many interviewees suggested an 'agile' methodology towards your early careers – trying things out but moving on quickly if it isn't the right fit.

Gertjan Rossing, Head of Strategy, CRM Partners, has this recommendation:

'Trying, analysing, improving, learning quickly and making mistakes. I think it is better to take the step, to commit mistakes and to learn from them rather than to sit at home, waiting and studying. If you compare it with cold calling prospects, you could prepare the cold call for an hour only to find out that it is the wrong guy. You need a balance. Of course, you need a bit of preparation, but over-preparing is not good either. I think it is better to learn quickly.'

KEY TAKEAWAY

Assess your strengths and weaknesses. Be sure to think long-term in your choice of roles but remember to be 'agile' in your approach.

Lesson 24: Your life stage and what you want

You can join sales anytime

Regardless of when you realise you want to go into sales, your life stage should not be a barrier. Sales was not a first job for over 25% of my interviewees, and many got into sales later in life.

Andrew Santos, CEO, Compass Group, believes life stage is not a factor when considering a sales career:

'If you have a few of these things that are kind of the key, the bread and butter, we can teach you the skill piece. It is just a trade. It is just a learnable thing. I do not think there is ever a bad time. In fact, I currently work with a lady who is sixty-seven years old. I worked with a gentleman who was seventy-two when he started. Age is just a number.'

Your family situation matters

Being an absolute top performer does require being relentlessly focused on your targets and goals though, potentially at the cost of your family life. John Schlegel, CEO, Stonebridge Search, says:

> 'Once you start having a family, things change. You can't think of it just for you any more, it becomes, "If I did that, it's going to affect them too. I know if it was just me, I could get lean. I can commit to what the ultimate outcome's going be – if I'm on my own, that's cool." I used to live on nothing; when we were selling door-to-door, we lived on $200 a week. You can do that if it's just you, but if it's a family it changes everything.'

Katrin Kieviselg, Partner, NorthStar Consulting, agrees:

> 'Being in the stage of life where I'm having children and building my family, I can still be successful, but I do not need to be number one at the top of the game all the time. I am really happy and grateful when I see junior people succeeding. They take all the knowledge from me and then they move to the next level and then they become number one, and that makes me proud. What I have sometimes seen is that when people get into the stage of having

children and creating a family, it is very difficult to figure out how can you be the number one dad and number one salesperson. You have to choose.'

It's about what you want

The company life stage you choose should ideally match your own (more on this in lesson 39). Julio Hernandez, CEO, EnLight.Energy, says:

> 'I think one thing that is not as popular to explore but has proven to be crucially important is timing. The level of sacrifice and the needs that are going be taken care of by an organisation in the first six months of operation are going be different from that of a three- or five-year-old business, and different than a twenty- or fifty-year-old company. Typically, the younger the company, the higher the possible reward, the higher the risk, the lower the certainty. Sometimes if this is misaligned you find that a person that would perform well in a different organisation underperforms when their needs and life stage are not a good match for the current stage of the company.'

KEY TAKEAWAY

Your life stage and establishing your priorities and your 'why' (lesson 1) are closely linked and need careful consideration to shape your desired role.

Lesson 25: Your first role is not forever

You make mistakes and you learn from them

While I've heard plenty of salespeople bemoan getting their first role wrong, many interviewees felt this was not an issue. Slim Earle of The Chemistry Group admits:

'I got it wrong in my first three jobs, I could not quite understand why but it felt wrong. I have since been able to reconcile why – whether it was the culture, the specifics of the role itself, the environment and the leadership, but I actually think there is still some value in going through those experiences.'

Rich Halbrooks, Vice President of Sales, McLeod Software, says:

'I would say that the first thing you want to do is work your way up selling other products. Much like I did, start off with a lower ticket item or something you can sell a little or a lot of or sell trial orders of. Then work your way up to larger ticket items and even larger ticket items until you get to the point where you're prepared to sell to a very narrow vertical market and be an expert.'

Have a formative experience

A significant amount of the interviewees recommended doing something incredibly tough as your first role, to make what comes after seem easy. Hans Keijmel, Strategic Account Director, Bloomreach, says:

'Start as a sales development representative, cold calling. That will not be the best period of your working life because there is a ton of stress. You have to follow exact principles to get things done. It is a really efficient way to one, understand the organisation; two, see the different roles within sales and in marketing; and three, to learn to work really hard.'

Roger Philby, CEO, The Chemistry Group, recommends a 'trial by fire' approach:

'This is going to sound incredibly old-fashioned, but find a job that is hell on earth and get forged in a crucible. Do not get bored in a really nice environment. My first job at Michael Page, I cold-called for half a day, every day. It was called a "calling hour" but we actually did it for longer. The lights would go out. We put orange flashing lights on and we just banged the phone. The point is not, "Did that teach me that it is a really good way of selling?" No. The productivity on it was awful. But does it mean that now I am prepared to pick up the phone to anyone without thinking about it, without having to sit there and say, "What script am I going to write and what should I talk about?" I am like, "Who do you want me to talk to?"'

KEY TAKEAWAY

In even the most complex industries, your first role will not define you (as in the next lesson). So, go big, go difficult or go for a high-growth environment that suits your interests, but don't worry too much about it.

Lesson 26: Consider your desired longevity at the company

Preferences for stability

Quite a few of my interviewees opted for long-term stability at their companies. Felipe Poveda, Head of Sales Europe, CreditSights, says:

'It depends what the goal is. If it's purely financial, I think there's a statistic that says if you move companies every two to three years, you get a higher base salary. Everyone has individual circumstances, but I don't think the financial element alone cuts it, because you can get paid handsomely without having to compromise on things like culture. It's just not worth it to do something that makes you unhappy.'

Manny Gonzalez, Financial Advisor, Raymond James, points out that building a sales career needs time:

> 'The biggest challenge that I see is when you start a brand-new career like this, it takes time to really develop it. The biggest challenge is, can you stick it out long enough to make it? Our industry has a 96% to 98% failure rate. Within the first five years, a brand-new advisor will probably not make it. That is the hard part, it is so difficult when you first get started, but once you've made it, it gets easier after that. It's kind of like pushing a train. It's very difficult to push the train, but once it gets going, man, that thing is hard to stop.'

It's OK to move at first

John Schlegel, CEO, Stonebridge Search, says:

> 'I would specifically say this (moving) is truer of people very early on in their careers. As a recruiter, you noticed people get passes for the first few years of their careers as they're trying to figure out what it is that they want to do. Now, once you get into years five, six, eight, ten-plus, you start getting less free passes from potential employers when they see that's happened.'

The longevity you should desire

Lots of managers did prefer previous job stability in their recruiting – which is a bit of a Catch-22, as those people are likely still with their previous companies.

Dimitry Toukhcher, CEO, LGFG Fashion House, puts it simply: 'It is not hard to recruit; it is just hard to recruit good people because bad people are always looking for jobs. They are always available. That is, by definition, the case.'

KEY TAKEAWAY

Regardless of whether you desire a single culture or to maximise your earnings in the short term, longevity is a significant career factor that merits consideration for both your current and future roles. (In lesson 89 there is some science explored in terms of when you should look to move.)

Lesson 27: There are 'finders, minders and grinders'

Definition and preference

My uncle, Jonathan Hamer, a retired law firm partner, explained to me:

'We used to talk about law firms as consisting of at least three types of people. You had your "finders", who were the people who went out and discovered the new clients; you had your "minders", which were the people who looked after clients and kept them happy; and then you had the "grinders", which were the people who did the work. A lot of law firms worked on the basis that "you ate what you killed". If you brought a deal in and it was worth a lot of money, then you got a lot of money that year and what that meant was the rainmakers – the ones that brought in deals – made a lot of money and the grinders didn't.'

By choosing sales you are ruling out the life of an internal grinder but there are some differences in the skillset and day-to-day work of the finder and the minder – often referred to as the hunter/farmer divide.

Greg Pearce, MD, Touchdown Charging, explains how he builds a team using the two styles:

'My type of selling is fast-paced. You can't just have go-getters and pitbull-style sellers, though. If you have two or three that are hard hustlers, then you have two or three that have more of a relationship style. I think it's important to have a blend of the two.'

Stuart Lotherington, MD, SBR Consulting, explores the hunter mentality:

'I think that there are definitely some people that are more suited to a hunter mentality. They like the chase. They like the hunt, the kill and the win.

Where those sorts of salespeople often let themselves down is that they do not build the relationships. They do not make sure to execute properly. They do not build the referrals you get back from a quality implementation process. They miss a trick because they are out to get the next thing, the next buzz and the next dopamine hit from all of the excitement.'

Distinctions in skillset

Alexei Bezborodov, Commercial Director, Lux Research, explains the different personality dynamics between the top account manager and new business hunter in his organisation:

'I was speaking with the account manager, and he's very good at understanding his client, really getting in deep and studying the organisation; understanding what the dynamics are, what the challenges are and then where the opportunities are. He's able to identify the needs and strategic opportunities for us to come in and offer things in a way that lands and delivers value. Whereas with my new business colleague, he's really good at challenging and getting people's attention. You need to get through the noise, you need to be able to really demonstrate that you are someone that you should pay attention to and really engage with the conversation. He has a similar ability to come up with a hypothesis and challenging question and ideas about what would really be valuable to the prospect. He shares this trait with the account manager, but there may be a little more aggressiveness, a little more persistence, a little more not taking "no" for an answer.'

You should ideally have both skills

In many organisations I've interviewed – particularly smaller organisations or those who take a 'land and expand' approach where a new business salesperson gets to keep an account they initially sell to – you can choose to be both a finder and a minder. John Willis, Director, 2Circles Communications, says:

> 'A good account manager is a good salesperson. A good salesperson is a good account manager. I don't think there is much distinction between the top performers in either category. If someone says, "I don't like having targets as an account manager," then they're the wrong guy for the account manager role. Someone could also say, "I don't like account management; I just want to sell." Then they're the wrong guy for sales too because sooner or later they will annoy people and lose clients.'

Phil Burgess, Chief People Officer, C Space, says:

> 'In the companies that I have been part of, I think the people that typically get to the top are able to hunt and farm. If you are running a

business, particularly in client services where revenue growth is always what you are ultimately measured on; to get to the top, you need to be on the hunt and win new business – both for the health of the business, but also to set an example. It is important to always be hungry. If you get too complacent and things get too good you can become a house cat, and you need to remember that you are a wild cat.'

KEY TAKEAWAY

Consider, at least early in your career, which technique might lead to easier success for you. As you progress you may find that both are good, but remember not to get complacent.

Lesson 28: Product complexity has value

The decision to be made on complexity

There's no doubt about it: if you are capable of selling complex products, you will be better valued and better paid. It's not for everyone, but focusing on a narrow, complicated vertical can reap some serious dividends if you start early.

Regarding financial sales, Chris Soprano, advisor, BondChain, notes:

'The reason these guys get compensated so well is that they have the intellectual capabilities to understand these financial instruments; to digest information and be able to sell them and adapt quickly. They also have social skills alongside this: to talk to people; to take them to dinner, to drinks; to build relationships. They are basically unicorns in that they have intellectual capability and social skills.'

Howard Paine, Regional Sales Manager, Zscaler, details the downsides and upsides of product complexity:

'I guess my description of complexity would be there's a lot of people involved, a lot of moving parts. They have an educational element; a bit of reframing is needed. There is a lot of stuff that needs doing with a lot of people, and it all needs to be coordinated to make something happen. I would recommend you learn how to sell complex products. If they need to hire people and you can make complex sales, they're going to be hiring the best people, and the better they'll look after you.'

You need to start early in some industries

To understand the complexities of your chosen field you do need to specialise fairly early. Brett Goodyear, Head of Sales EMEA, Challenger Inc, puts a time limit on that decision:

'I think you probably need to get into it in your first ten years because I think if you don't, there's a risk that people have expectations of expertise that are not fair to someone who hasn't accumulated that experience. So, I'd say the first ten years of your career anybody can step into complex sales.'

Owen Rothe, Relationship Manager, Lord, Abbett & Co, muses:

'I think it is probably fair to say that if you look at career trajectories of people in my role or similar roles in this industry, they are pretty much lifers in the industry, especially if you find success. Maybe they did something funky for a couple of years right out of school, but nowadays this is even rare because of how specialised everyone is getting in college.'

KEY TAKEAWAY

Product complexity is a specialised field, and it's becoming more so. Get in early if your passion (or passion for profit) is in a complex field. Either way, modern salespeople should look to own a specific vertical (lesson 94) at some point in their careers.

Lesson 29: Tangible vs intangible sales

When I sold educational books door-to-door, one of the things we were taught was to put the books into someone's hands. If something is physical, it's clear what the need is and they can see and feel their need to buy. That's not true in intangible sales, which adds a variety of difficulties and upsides to the sales process.

Both types have value

Stuart Lotherington, MD, SBR Consulting, says:

> 'I think when you start in sales, it is quite nice to have a tangible product. It is going to be a much easier sell, but I think the challenge in our world is that a lot of things are becoming commoditised. Recent data is that around 80% of people will check prices online now, so if you are selling a commoditised product, if people are able to get the same thing somewhere else for cheaper, then it does not make any economic sense to buy.
>
> 'You might be able to add value somehow in the sales process, but the demand and the growth of online activity shows that people are looking at it for context. You need to look at the longer-term game. "Will I have a job and will I be selling this product, or will it be commoditised?" The exciting thing about conceptual selling is that it is much harder – you have got to base it on so much more

than just saying what you are offering. Conceptual selling is going to stand the test of time, and the contract values can be very large. If you are in a commission environment and you are selling large-scale projects, for example, that would be pretty exciting.'

Tangible product considerations

John Schlegel, CEO, Stonebridge Search, tells the story of his friend who left recruitment for physical product sales:

> 'He said, "I'm young, and this isn't going to get any easier. I'm gonna try something different now. I really feel like I need a tangible product to sell, where it is a formulaic, much more structured situation." He did that and it worked great and now he's doing fantastically well. I mean, he's one of the best people in the country for this particular medical device he sells. He needed to have the benefits of a core set of products memorised. He needed to know what type of people buy them and he needed to be able to set up a very regimented schedule to go out and sell that. He is a very organised, detailed, structured guy.'

Intangible product considerations

Intangible products have the added difficulty of being more complex and having more potential objections.

Personally, the toughest thing I found about intangible products was driving urgency with customers. Ronald Sluiter, Global Director, Gartner, agrees:

'Why should we start collaborating tomorrow, and not in two or three months? That is very hard because we sell knowledge. It is pretty hard for people to see it and feel it, and to see the personal value, which drives urgency.'

Anne-Marie Lee, Senior Manager, Aviva, feels that a belief in intangible products is necessary for success:

'I think success depends on the ability to understand insurance and develop a belief in it. It's not like selling property or selling books, which are easier sales because you can touch them. You can feel them. You can see them. If you're a really good salesperson and you think selling books is too little money, you can sell a bigger object that's also tangible. I think with insurance, if you don't believe in it, then it's probably going to be difficult to persevere because you will face objections.'

Mike Turner, MD, YouBecome, muses:

'I've been running a consultancy business for the last fifteen years and sometimes rue the day that I chose to sell consulting rather than a nice tangible product because back in the days selling books you had a product, and you sold the product. Someone could see it, someone could turn the pages and look at it, whereas, effectively, I'm selling an idea as a consultant. It's a big difference, and I'm also selling my reputation.'

KEY TAKEAWAY

While there are advantages to both types of products, intangible products tend to be higher margin (lesson 33) and selling them can make you more valuable as a salesperson so if the added challenge doesn't put you off, choosing this route merits consideration.

Lesson 30: Choose your length of cycle

Length of sales cycles

When I joined Gartner, the S&P 500 advisory firm, I was told that I wouldn't make a new business sale for at least three months, and more likely six. I'd been used to more fast-paced sales where I might close three or four deals a month. Of course, I scoffed at it taking that long and planned on setting records for speed. I put my head down, worked hard, followed the process... and closed my first deal five and a half months later.

Rhys Zownir, Business Development Manager, React News, highlights the key difference between sales cycle length:

'The biggest difference is risk. Long sales cycles inherently carry more risk because there's more time that someone can drop out at any period. If you're selling to someone and it's a twelve-month sales cycle, it's much easier to not hit your target because of the length of the sales cycle, and you're going to put in more time and more effort as that cycle progresses.'

The cycle skillsets differ

Nazma Qurban, CRO, Cognism, shares his experience:

'I have had experiences where we went from a very short sales cycle and commitment to a much longer one while growing the team organically. I would say looking at other organisations, they would have an expectation that somebody has a certain skillset. If it is a long-term contract, they are really good at creating relationships; they are consultative; and they have a lot more patience. The skillset would be different in high-volume sales, how they actually communicate and deliver the proposition becomes more important.'

The difference in two recruiters – one who chose short-cycle, and one long-cycle – is telling. Corbin McGuire, MD, RNM Recruiting, prefers the short-cycle:

'I'm not the best person to talk about in a long sales cycle because I think that they're so low energy there. I've never been able to do that or teach it or play in that and as a result I end up doing lots more smaller deals. The smaller deals that I do are easier to do, quicker to do, but they create more energy. I could be so much more productive in creating more dollars if I would just do bigger deals.'

Rusty Branch, CEO, Compass Law, specialises in the long game:

'You could shoot for a year and not have killed anything, but you're really, really doing a good job. You haven't brought a cent of revenue into the firm, but boy, you're killing it. That takes a unique personality to build, understand and appreciate where that's coming from. I can go six months without bringing any money in, but I'm able to go calculate all the smaller steps and know exactly what each stage is worth.'

KEY TAKEAWAY

Are you more patient, team oriented, formal and willing to take on more risk? Or do you prefer the fast pace, simplicity and energy of shorter, more transactional sales? Your career trajectory should follow suit.

Lesson 31: One-sided markets are simpler but two can pay more

What's needed

A number of interviewees, particularly in the fields of placing financial services employees (legal, consulting, engineering, tech and sales) and in finance, had to create their own markets, ie they needed to procure a buyer and a seller to create a sale.

Chris Soprano, advisor, BondChain, recalls his previous sales careers:

> 'Brokers create something from nothing. Usually, salespeople have something to sell so there is less creativity involved: "OK, I have this widget and I want to sell it to you." Whereas brokers, they don't have an inventory; they have to create something from nothing. It's all about supply and demand. One of your clients has some demand and you have to go find the other side, which is the supply side, and vice versa. With the salesperson, the minute he gets asked about supply and demand, he goes to somebody else and tries to find it.'

Charles Talbot, MD, Pinpoint Partners, explains:

> 'In recruitment you've got to negotiate managing both sides because you've got humans as the commodities on both ends. There are added nuances. You'll go from one to the other. It can be super easy

on one side and then it's completely the other way around. And that's completely evolving.'

A good reason to choose two-sided

Denee Siddall, Account Manager, Deverell Smith, gets at the incentive for choosing a two-sided market, comparing external (two-sided) to internal (single company) recruitment:

> 'I think it's definitely tougher but the fees that we charge are a lot higher – you can make double in external recruitment. It's a challenging role; people in external recruitment turn over much more often. That is all about relationship-building and strategising and spreadsheets.'

KEY TAKEAWAY

People who want to do two-sided sales need a variety of organisational and soft skills but if you can handle it, choosing a two-sided market can be a lucrative choice.

5
Lessons On Industry Considerations

'Selling something you don't believe in, I truly hope that neither you nor anyone else finds out how to do that, because if they do, I'm not sure that they're adding anything to the sum of human happiness.'
— Simon Ruddick, Chairman, Albourne Partners

Lesson 32: Try and follow your passion

Finding your passion

If you can find your passion and you don't mind turning it into a job, you should go for it. Many of the interviewees were passionate about what they do.

Scott Roy, CEO, Whitten & Roy, gives this advice:

'I think one thing I would do is choose a company that sells something you believe in. I just had a sales meeting this morning with a woman here in

Nairobi and she asked me the question, "Why are you doing this rather than working in London and making a lot more money?" I said, "You know, I'm sixty-two years old; I want to do something that makes a difference and I know what my company and I do makes a huge difference in people's lives – for both the buyers and the sellers. If we can teach fifty to sixty organisations a year how to be great at selling, they're going make a pretty good size dent in issues around poverty and I'm happy about that.'

Kristen Gonzalez of Thrive positively beams when she talks about her job:

'I'd rather message someone about Thrive. I'd rather call somebody and tell them what it is doing for me and what it could possibly do for them like my soul is on fire. I just want to tell every single person about it and my passion is so sky-high that I want to spend every minute doing sales.'

Passion for what you do creates energy

There is a pragmatism in passion for what you do, as well. Corbin McGuire, MD, NDM Recruiting, notes:

'People will say, "You need to go follow your passion," but what they're really communicating is, "Go where you get energy because if you get energy it will lead to lots of repetitions." Once we hit rep number nine-million-two-hundred, or whatever, we become an expert at it. In sales, you're getting rejected, you are alone and the energy can be non-existent and discouraging. That shuts down reps, and when reps shut down, your ability to capture data and learn shuts down. Reps equal success, and reps come from energy and passion.'

What to do if you don't have a passion

Not everyone has a specific passion for the industry they're in, but you do need to have a passion for an aspect of what you do – whether that be the people (lesson 16) or the results of your profits. Howard Paine, Regional Sales Manager, Zscaler, says:

'What I try to give myself is the ability to give back and look after my family, and it also gives you other opportunities to influence stuff. In fact, the first two bosses I've worked for in sales were both great and ultimately both did really cool stuff for charity. They used their resources to do some pretty cool stuff.'

Chris Soprano, advisor, BondChain, has this advice:

'What I always tell people, especially younger people, is if you have a passion in your life, then pursue it. If you don't have a passion but the financial world is a place where you can get the most remuneration, then that makes sense too. If your passion does not give you enough money for a vacation, then find a job that can pay you the most money that it can for your vacation. In your spare time, you can follow that passion that you have as a hobby.'

KEY TAKEAWAY

Follow your passion or follow the money that can lead to your passion, but ensure that you're excited about some aspect of the industry or the company you choose to enter.

Lesson 33: The upside of bigger package sizes

It's challenging and fulfilling

While selling bigger deals is more difficult and requires a longer sales cycle (lesson 30), it certainly has its upsides. Rick Halbrooks, VP Sales, McLeod Software, says:

'Certainly, the rewards are greater when you're selling bigger ticket items. You have to have a more complicated sale, a more high-level sale and so you need to hire only the very best salespeople. We're not hiring people like I did when I was in the photocopier business for years, where we were hiring kids coming straight out of college or people who were wanting to get their foot in the door in the sales field. We are hiring folks who have had tremendously successful sales careers already, who want to go to the next level where they can sell larger ticket items, more complicated sales where they get paid more money. It's more fulfilling when you can go home and say, "I closed a million-and-a-half-dollar deal today," as compared to, "I closed a $7,000 dollar deal today."'

Higher margins are better paid and more fun

In my experience product margin and profitability have been the biggest factors in determining a salesperson's enjoyment and take-home pay. John Schlegel, CEO, Stonebridge Search, says:

'I have seen people that I genuinely believe are more talented, but other people are quadrupling them in earnings because they're choosing to sell something that has a very low margin and a very low ticket size. I would encourage young salespeople to think about this, as well as their chosen field.'

John also tells a story of how a friend chose his industry:

'He didn't care what he sold theoretically. He was not emotionally attached to anything, and he determined that selling medical equipment devices had a high yield of what he could make. He was considering that versus pharmaceutical drug sales and a couple of other things. He literally made his choice based on the maths of what's possible within those businesses, and his lifestyle as a result.'

I experienced this in perhaps my biggest career move to date – moving from a low-margin, high-volume, low-deal-sized world in P&G to an extremely high-margin, medium-deal size at Debtwire. I almost instantly doubled my earnings, had unlimited earning potential, a relatively unscrutinised client expense account, and more regular team outings.

KEY TAKEAWAY

When businesses make more money, they tend to spend more of it on their salesforce so look out for higher margin businesses. Big deal sizes and high margins are the pinnacle of profitability if you can find such a company and get your foot in the door.

Lesson 34: Residuals are great to sell

Benefits

If a business has residual income, both the business and its salespeople are usually better valued. John Willis, Director, 2Circles Communications, speaks about telecoms:

'The lifetime value of every client that you bring on board is huge because a lot of the services are repeat revenue-based and there are lots of different solutions within the same overall solution. That makes clients very sticky as well. To get it right is extremely important and the value of a client is high, which means that you need to compensate salespeople accordingly.'

Theo Davies, Head of Cloud Sales Enablement JAPAC, Google, says:

'They have higher residuals in insurance, for example, because you build a wall of income. The residual income is the main difference and having that wall means they will be keen to deploy a percentage into training their agents and brokers to sell better. It's a vested interest. For every sale they make, the company makes thirty years of income.'

Many miss the benefit of residuals

The lack of residual revenue was a common regret for those who don't have it. Corbin McGuire reflects, 'I would have done a sales job that had a re-occurring revenue stream versus one-time fees. An insurance agent receives renewals. A head-hunter doesn't.'

Hugo Barclay, Owner, ArtThou, says:

'I think the worst thing in art is the lack of residual income. It is a one-off transaction, so someone can buy a painting and that is great. You can get to a place where you have developed a relationship where you think that they are loyal to you, but there is nothing saying that they really are.'

KEY TAKEAWAY

If you can, choose a residual income industry, and make sure you're paid on those residuals. Insurance, telecoms, advisory, media and tech are just some examples of where you can find that benefit.

Lesson 35: Market timings and niches

Following trends

Learning to recognise trends won't necessarily make you a good salesperson, but it is a useful skill to develop. Rakesh Patel, Founder, Product Freedom, gives an example of an emerging trend:

> 'So many businesses use Xero now. What is the benefit of creating the transaction in your firm and having some accountant shift boxes; you put that into a different box; and then submit that to the government? It wouldn't surprise me if there are no more standard accountants in ten years. Tech is going to be hugely disruptive over the next ten to fifteen years.'

Avi Weisenberg, CRO and startup advisor, says:

> 'You can choose your career and become the world's greatest expert on widgets. You can build your career around that. The challenge with that is that you have to make sure that you are in an industry that is big enough and future-proof enough, which probably isn't widgets. You need both passion and foresight in your career to be successful.'

Committing to a niche

Hugo Barclay, Owner, ArtThou, says:

> 'I would focus on product categories first. I'd probably get trained at tech sales and then I think I would also look at location. So, I mean if I am in the UK, I would go to London; or in the States, the Bay Area or Austin or New York – big cities that are known for that industry. I would do that specifically to allow myself to generate more luck – by generating more luck, I mean being in a place where I can meet the main people within the industry that I am working in and also being able to network as much as possible. I think that location is really important to the beginning of your career.'

Market timings

In choosing an industry and product, you also need to be aware of whether that product will become defunct. Lauri Kinkar, CEO, Messente Communications, gives this advice:

'If I were to choose a company as a young salesperson, I would look at the product and the value. The best companies are those whose product is in a very good position five years from now, and obviously not in a declining market. If you are selling something that the demand for is already slowly declining, it is a no-brainer, just get out. But if you are at a point where the world has not caught up with the value that this product might provide, that's a great place to be.'

KEY TAKEAWAY

With the rapid change of technology within industries and sales (lesson 99), it would benefit a salesperson to study trends and market dynamics that might benefit them and to orient their careers accordingly.

Lesson 36: Your network is a career opportunity

Network marketing has increasing prominence

If you network well (lesson 80) it can be a prospecting and sales goldmine. No form of selling to your network is more direct than the trend towards network marketing, the social selling of products or services to your peer group and friends.

Kristen Gonzalez, VIP Brand Promoter, Thrive, is a network marketing savant:

> 'It's everywhere now. Five hundred thousand people join network marketing a month globally. I think it's our future. I mean it's been around for a while but it's shaping up and now there are better companies, better leaders and it's desirable. People want to live their life and also make money, especially Millennials, but it could be anybody. Instagram influencers are network marketers. I think it can be a full-time or a part-time career but it can't be a "sometime". What I mean is you can do it full time, you can do it part time, but I think you can't just decide to "tell some people about it today". Wishy-washy isn't going to help you make the sale. It has to be consistent. I worked up to the third rank in the company while I was working full-time and coaching and with all the other things going on, because I put in the work consistently.'

Helen Bee, CEO, Clean Living International, details the trend she's seeing in network marketing:

> 'You basically choose what you want to earn and when you want to work, and it is your responsibility then as an independent business owner to make that happen. Nobody is on your back managing you at all. So it is more about when people start to apply the learning and listening to the best practice that is shared, when they start applying that and go, "Oh, gosh, this works." That is when that lightbulb moment normally comes, when going from a part-time into a full-time role.'

Reversing the stigma and being comfortable with it

Kristen Gonzalez, VIP Brand Promoter, Thrive, is the first to admit that network marketing has a stigma which exceeds that of normal sales:

> 'People are just sceptical of the industry. They think it's a scam. And unfortunately, network marketing in the past has had some negatives. Things happened – either the companies weren't ethical or maybe the products weren't that great. So, the current companies that are doing it, people think it's a scam, a pyramid scheme. As for pyramid schemes, my last career in teaching was a pyramid scheme; I wasn't going to make more than what the principal was making, then if I became principal, the

superintendent made more than her, so I feel you actually have more flexibility in network marketing than other careers.'

Helen Bee, CEO, Clean Living International, agrees:

'The worst and most unfair element of it is the stigma attached to it. It never ever ceases to amaze me that there are some people who have a real ignorance and are almost determined not to just give it a chance and listen to it. They are just so quick to shut you down and want to go, "It is a pyramid scheme. It is a scam," when, in truth, they do not really know what a pyramid scheme is. It can really open people's eyes when they look at how well people do in network marketing, and when they learn how big a contributor it is to the economy overall.'

You need to always be closing

Kristen Gonalez goes on to explain a recent interaction with her bank teller:

'I saw her drinking a coffee – drinking coffee in the afternoon! I was like, "Boom." I've learned to capitalise on the moment. I knew there was a need right there because I could tell that she was tired in the afternoon. I just asked her if she had ever heard about Thrive and she hadn't. I explained to her how it helped. I knew what her need was, so I filled that – "It helps with energy; it helps with focus." I knew she was around people all day and crunching numbers. I told her a story of how it's helped my husband in his career with numbers and people. I just capitalised on that moment and the excitement. She was right at the buying point. Why would I let that go? I'm not going to wait to go back and follow up with her later. I'm going to capitalise at that point.'

KEY TAKEAWAY

The mentality of always being ready to sell and looking for prospects can be lucrative and allow for a huge amount of freedom and flexibility in what you do. Many salespeople have started network marketing as a side-hustle and developed it into highly lucrative full-time jobs so this may be an alternative route to consider.

Lesson 37: Some industries don't have traditional sales

Non-traditional sales industries

While the industry considerations so far have related to sales roles, it's important to note that some industries (especially law and most varieties of banking or consulting) don't have traditional sales roles. This results in a strange dynamic where 'business development' professionals are not responsible for their own targets, but instead support the senior technical experts to sell their services.

Consultancy and law as examples

Jonathan Hamer, ex-partner of an Australian law firm, says:

> 'You didn't get made a partner until you had done grinder work for a long time and established yourself as a person who was a safe pair of hands to perform a minder role. In rare cases you may have become recognised as a leader in an area of expertise so that making you a partner would enable you to better attract work. Essentially, what we generated was a team inside the law firm who were basically the public relations and whose role would be organising and assisting the partners to be minders and finders rather than just grinders.' (Lesson 25 defines finders, minders and grinders.)

Alastair Ross, Owner, Codexx Associates, recalls his first sales experience in consulting:

> 'It's still fresh in my memory – the first sales call when I was a junior consultant back at IBM in about '92, and I was too scared to go on my own. I asked a colleague to come with me to see the managing director of an electronics business. It's good to look back on that because you forget. You sort of think, "How on earth could anybody be worried about it?" I think looking at the sales role – you can't call them a client if you can't sell to them. Building up your confidence in the ability to have a credible discussion with the client is key. I think what I

was worried about is whether I knew enough. Was I going to be placed in a situation where I'd ask a stupid question or not understand what the client said? That was me right at my beginning as I developed within consulting.'

Sales skills are always needed

Even in these types of industries, sales skills will inevitably pay off. They can lead you to different career paths, potentially morphing into a sales career in the long run. Charles Talbot, MD, Pinpoint Partners, says:

'Clearly if you join a sales team you are in a sales role, but you can also secure a role where you are a technical practitioner initially, but in due course, your role evolves into a sales role. For example, an accountant, a banker, a lawyer, a consultant – as you get more senior, your role becomes sales-focused because you sell to win business.'

Rupa Datta, Owner, Portfolio People, agrees:

'I've certainly seen cases where people have had technical expertise before they go into sales – certainly mid-career professionals in engineering and computing. That's when they realised that technically they're very good and functionally they're very good, but for them to go to director level they need to go into sales, and that becomes its own career path.'

Neil Checker, Senior Advisor, Arthur D Little, says:

> 'It is quite clear that you progress faster in consulting, especially in a partnership structure, if you can exhibit early on the ability to build client relationships and bring in business – that fact is clear. In many consulting firms, if you are not capable of doing that, then your career is going to be quite limited. Even as a consultant during delivery of the project, day to day, you have to try to identify where the firm's services can be beneficial to the client and then work with senior colleagues to develop, and hopefully sell, that capability.'

KEY TAKEAWAY

There are a few lessons here. If you are determined to go into these industries, you should be aware it might be a while before you are actually in sales. Likewise, if you go into these industries to sell, be aware that the usual benefits of quantifying your impact (lesson 17), and great variable pay (lesson 22), might not be there. Lastly, regardless of the industry you end up in, sales skills will be necessary to become exceptional at some point.

Lesson 38: Going entrepreneurial is always an option

Entrepreneurialism goes further than sales

This is not specifically a book about entrepreneurialism, but with so many brilliant entrepreneurs interviewed on sales, and sales skills consistently being recommended as necessary to become an entrepreneur, it's impossible not to touch on the best quotes on the subject. Simon Ruddick, Chairman, Albourne Partners, says:

> 'If you're not that kind of person, I don't think people can talk themselves into being an entrepreneur. If you're not, chances are you'll miss out to someone else who has that higher level of insanity. I've never achieved any high-level sport, but when you hear things like Wayne Rooney or David Beckham doing a million hours of taking free kicks, you realise there's someone out there with an obsession. Entrepreneurship is very different from sales. Entrepreneurship is the compulsion you can't turn off. It's an itch you can never scratch. It's just something you have to do because you are obsessed, compelled and driven by a vision of how things can be.'

Amanda Derham, Director, The Agile Director, describes what is needed in entrepreneurs:

> 'Commitment, passion, and grit because the road is very long and lonely and you need extraordinary

grit to keep going. Also, an ability to get out of the setbacks, because there will be enormous setbacks. And you need to have the personality. And a lot of that is absolute doggedness. That is an entrepreneur's secret sauce, but also their worst enemy, because often they do not know when to quit. And sometimes, it is both the best thing about an entrepreneur and the worst.'

The crossover between sales and entrepreneurialism

John Schlegel, CEO, Stonebridge Search, shares his opinion:

'To me, entrepreneurialism is basically sales. I created my own firm because it didn't make sense long-term to be a part of a bigger company doing what I do. I think that might be unique to recruiting, because what I'm finding is that a lot of companies that I recruit for are used to much bigger agencies. In my case it's myself, maybe one assistant, and that's all that's required. A lot of my friends end up starting their own firm. So, for me, it's been very closely connected.'

Upsides and downsides

Nick Beresford, CEO, Enertor, highlights one of the challenges in choosing the entrepreneurial route:

'They always say that there's never a really good time to start your own business. You're either too young and too inexperienced with no money; and then in the middle of your life you've got a lot of cash needs, you've got kids that you're trying to educate or whatever it is. When you finish that you're too old, so there's never a good time from a life point of view.'

Richard Humphreys, ex-CEO, Saatchi & Saatchi, believes it is worth it:

'Who succeeds in the long run? I would say generally the entrepreneurs. If I look around at people who are, in my view, successful on the business side, it's the people who have done their own thing, not necessarily people who have gone from being the junior guy on the biggest account on earth and then worked their way up to be a medium guy, etc.'

KEY TAKEAWAY

Having been part of the team that started a profitable business in React News, I have two pieces of advice to offer. One is to surround yourself with brilliant people – ideally partners and mentors. The other is to listen for what your potential clients are asking you for most often (in our case, quality real estate news).

6

Lessons On Company Considerations

'I would say it is very important that you can honestly and quickly explain why you want to work with a company. If you can't explain it well to your mother or your father, please think about it again. I think that is important because if you like the company, its values and its services, and if you really believe in it, it is easier to sell. And if you can't explain it, try harder or don't apply.'

— Gertjan Rossing, Head of Delivery, CRM Partners

Lesson 39: Choosing the company life stage

Large or small company considerations

There are benefits to larger corporations in terms of process (lesson 64) and internal training (lesson 45). Smaller companies benefit from direct access to leadership (lesson 50) and a high-growth culture (lesson 42).

Which you choose is a personal preference. Carolin Berger, Regional Sales Director, Outpost 24, says:

> 'I know I would much rather be in a smaller company where I have a lot of responsibility and can take decisions instead of being in a big organisation where I have a fancy title but I actually have no authority because there are a thousand different roles.'

Charles Talbot, MD, Pinpoint Partners, prefers bigger companies:

> 'I would probably reflect that actually I am a more corporate guy than I thought. If I had it again, I would probably take the slightly longer option in a bigger organisation at the start of my career, but you would have never convinced me to do that as a young guy coming out of university. I thought I could run before I could walk, I thought life was short and getting it all done by the age of twenty-five was super important.'

Startup considerations

Startups are also an option, with more extreme upsides and downsides. Howard Paine, Regional Sales Manager, Zscaler, says:

> 'I think those kinds of companies attract the best kind of people and I believe that you are a product of the ten people you spend the most of your time

with. These companies seem to be full of brilliant people. They are taking all the best because they are growing quick enough to fund their requirements.'

Nazma Qurban, CRO, Cognism, has encountered difficulties when working for startups:

'You also have to perceive yourself as not being a startup, because I think one of the biggest misconceptions that I had when I started off was, "Oh, yeah. People love to buy from startups." No! Nobody loves buying from startups. It is such a huge risk. Why would somebody do that?'

Startups have the benefit of lean decision-making and high growth, but it takes a certain type of risk-taker to stomach that additional company-based risk.

Consider the company ownership

Having worked in businesses owned by investors who wanted steady growth (P&G), high growth (Gartner) and exponential growth (React News), I have recognised what an important a driver ownership is in an organisation.

Carolin Berger, Regional Sales Manager, Outpost 24, shares her experience:

'The company I work in right now is backed by private equity. That is a luxurious situation created because our investors are long-term investors. But sometimes there are those notorious venture capital funds and you read about how long they keep a company and how poorly they treat their staff.'

KEY TAKEAWAY

Make sure that the ownership and corporate ambition of a company match what you want at every stage of your career.

Lesson 40: Product and Porter's Five Forces

Porter's Five Forces

One of the few things that stuck with me from my financial exams was the concept of the 'Porter's Five Forces' model.[9] It is a simple way to think of the factors that most affect company performance and identifies the five key potential barriers to profitability. They are:

1. The bargaining power of suppliers

2. The threat of new entrants

3. The threat of substitute products

---

9   ME Porter, 'How competitive forces shape strategy', *Harvard Business Review*, (May 1979), 57(2), pp137–145

4. The bargaining power of product buyers

5. Industry rivalry

I'd encourage you to scrutinise your potential company and its product with these factors in mind.

Product considerations

Saj Samiullah, Director, Quantribute, shares this advice:

> 'Whatever role you go for, do a lot of research up front. That'll determine how hard your life is going to be. Are the leads generated automatically, or are you going to generate them yourself? Do they have a marketing machine where Google rankings work for them? Does the company have an antiquated view of sales? Are their competitors doing things better or in a more modern way? Is the company at the forefront of technology, and can they survive in a digital age?'

Radoslav Ivanov, International Sales Executive, Historical Park Bulgaria, recently read a book called *Blue Ocean Strategy: How to create uncontested market space and make competition irrelevant.*[10] It helped him to determine a strategy in light of the threat of new entrants:

---

10 W Chan Kim and R Mauborgne, *Blue Ocean Strategy: How to create uncontested market space and make competition irrelevant* (Gildan Media, 2006)

'I understood that if I am going to go into an industry in sales, or if I want to build a company of my own, I would want to have a market where nobody else can compete with me. It's the same for other entrepreneurs – if they want to have something and be number one in the world, they have to have something so unique that they can protect it.'

What you sell may or may not be unique, but it does have to have advantages over competition – in superiority or in price – to make it worth you selling it.

Market leaders or disruptors

Is it more fun to work for a market leader or a disruptor? Both sides were argued for by our interviewees, but organisations which were strongly one or the other were certainly preferred to the middle ground.

Richard Kiddle, Director, Titanbay, says:

'In terms of a product, I think I would look for something that is established and has a really good track record, where you are going in and you know what you are getting. Otherwise, I would go in for the more high-risk product and you can grow aggressively and be a part of that from the beginning. I've done the two ends of the spectrum and now I would personally not look for anything in the middle ground. I think either I want to be working with a market leader or I want to be working with something that is hardly known and get the opportunity to build that.'

KEY TAKEAWAY

There are a lot of different factors which can weaken a company and make your sales more difficult, but Porter's Five Forces are one way to structure your thinking. Figure out what you want and go for it, preferably avoiding middle-ground companies who are neither market leaders nor disruptors.

Lesson 41: Choose your organisational goals and values

Organisational goals

Some of the most exciting (and conversely, unexciting) places I have worked at were determined by the levels of clarity and ambition of their shared team goals.

Anthony Charlton, Commercial Director, Gartner, discusses how to get teams pulling together on shared goals:

'At base level, it is about sharing the number goal with the entire team and getting people to strive to that. Lay that out clearly, be transparent in what that number is and make it visual. Whether you slap it on the walls or create some other sort of visual representation, it should be out there. When you have your number and your prize, get people hyped up about it, telling them that this is the one thing we need to win as a team. Having that sort of an incentive and the team buying into that as a prize can make the business spike across that period and cause huge overachievement.'

Nick Beresford, CEO, Enertor, says:

'The whole idea of setting big team goals is that people can get excited about it and because it stretches everything. It stretches the team and it stretches the individuals to do things that they probably wouldn't have thought about and to give huge sales pitches or business plans rather than a few points of incremental growth. For me that was one of the frustrations about P&G – it was built on Wall Street, which needs 3% or 4% growth year-on-year and doesn't really need anything more than that.'

My favourite organisational goal was set by Nick at P&G. Our sales channel (basically the 'other' channels that weren't the declining major supermarkets) was worth about £350m in 'NOS' (a proxy for profit) at the time and Nick was determined to get it to £500m within three years – a huge goal deemed unlikely by others in the organisation. Nick set up a pyramid of £1m 'bricks'. Each time a team member contributed an additional £1m profit, a brick was added to the wall. The entire team – perhaps myself especially – took huge pleasure and pride in placing these bricks.

When we finally accomplished this goal (nine months early) there was a party involving a Scottish castle and fireworks, the like of which is rarely seen at P&G. It was a seminal moment in my career and convinced me that I always want to be part of huge, shared goals.

Values

Much like organisational goals, your values also need to align with the organisation you apply to work for. Jason Dial, Chairman, LGFG Fashion House, highlights his value-based interview technique:

> 'Where do you see this business going? You should be asking the same questions that they are asking you. What is the goal of this company? What is your five-year plan? If they do not have an answer, I would be worried. I have had two jobs in twenty-one years, and when I came over, I specifically asked my business partner, "What is the plan?" If he had said, "Make a lot of money," then we would have had an issue, but he was specific with where we are going and what we are building, and it is a lot easier to get on board with that. People want to be on board with successful people.'

Robin Mukherjee, MD, 2Circles Consulting, says:

> 'It's a very personal thing. It's a bit like a relationship and you want to find an organisation and partner in life that has got the same values as you

do. When the values are aligned, then that's when you have a really good match.'

KEY TAKEAWAY

Plenty of salespeople struggle on with their goals and values not matched by, or even at odds with, those of their organisations. Try and find a match with goals and values that inspire you.

Lesson 42: Culture is honestly huge

Definitions of culture

Culture is an enormous topic, so let's make it more tangible. In simple terms, culture is defined by an organisation's workforce and how they behave. Lars Tewes, Director, Clean Living International, defines culture as such:

> 'I believe that culture is basically the behaviour of the people in that business. It is not about reading their website values and various statements. Culture is based on people's behaviour and you cannot hide that – from how you are greeted at reception through to dealing with the accounts payable department.'

Mike Turner, Owner, YouBecome, has a more comprehensive definition of culture, with six clear pillars:

'Trust and empowerment is the first one. The second one is a quality leadership team that are united, they think in the same way and they point in the same direction and are very approachable and open. The third one is a business that's customer obsessed. "How do we keep them? How do we take care of them?" They decide based on customer requirements rather than their own. The fourth one is very much around professional and personal development. It's how we are going to help every single individual in this business be better at their jobs over the next six to twelve months, whether that's through encouragement, kicking, whatever it might be. The fifth is communication. Brilliant communication from the top down; allowing people to communicate up the chain whether they're happy or not. Then the final one is what we call a growth attitude, which is a sense that, "We're all in this together. We're trying to get better as a company. We're trying to provide better products, and we're trying to be better at what we do." If a business demonstrates those qualities, then they are the top of their business. I'm lucky enough to have worked with a few, but it's rare.'

You Become's six pillars of culture

The upsides and downsides

Rhys Zownir, Business Development Manager, React News, has experienced both good and bad culture:

'If the culture is that brilliant, then I really think it no longer seems like work. Even if you're doing something which is a bit of a rubbish task during the week, if it's a great culture, it's still fun in a weird way because you're just doing it around people that you like and get along with. If you're working in a terrible culture, it's kind of the antithesis of what I just described – if it's a terrible culture, then no one wants to be there, and everyone's looking on LinkedIn for the first opportunity to get out of there.'

Rich Kiddle, Director, Titanbay, shares his experience of a poor culture fit:

'I quickly learned that the culture was not for me. It was very tense, with people working out of fear rather than because they wanted to perform. It was very much about the time spent at your desk rather than about output and performance. People were not very happy, moaning all the time in the office, and it affected the health of the staff. People were not working together. I thought there were a lot of things going on behind the scenes that we did not know about and then you found out at a later date that one person was getting this, and the business is doing that – you had no idea. For me now, it's about knowing everyone is on the same page.'

Testing the waters

Culture is clearly important, so how do you test for it before joining an organisation? Mark Cooper, Owner, Cooper and Lansbury Associates, argues that you need access to the office to determine culture:

'Culture is huge, and I will stand in any open-plan office and have a look around, and I just know within five minutes whether this is a good place to work or whether it's not. I would love to be able to say there is something scientific around that, and to talk about the "percentage of smile", but it's just little things – you get a feel for it. It's the way people talk to each other; it's the buzz around the office that suggests whether or not people have fun while working there.'

Helen Bee, CEO, Clean Living International, concurs:

> 'Even in interview stages, you can see the culture from the type of environment that they have, the welcome that you will get from walking through the door. There are some real tell-tale signs. Do they take the time to really get to know you? Do they make you feel at ease, make you feel relaxed and understand what you are trying to get out of the role or out of the purchase? There were some key things that jump out for me even before you get the employee handbook or the marketing brochure. You can get a feel for what they are all about and what their true intent is from having that initial interaction with you.'

Felipe Poveda, Head of Sales EMEA, CreditSights, gives this advice:

> 'If you ask a question and you feel like people are holding back or just giving you generalisations then you kind of have to probe into what they're saying. What do they mean by, "Management are really approachable," or, "It's a really flat structure," or, "People enjoy themselves together outside of work"? I think if a company has a good culture, they will take the opportunity to answer the question with a lot of specific stories or examples of their most recent shared experiences which define who they are. If they have nothing else to say, maybe it's because there is nothing else to tell you.'

KEY TAKEAWAY

An organisation's culture has a huge impact on the quality of your work experience, so do some research before accepting new roles and consider whether you'll be a good fit.

Lesson 43: Find somewhere that celebrates sales success

The risk of not celebrating

For most people, the level of recognition received is crucial to their performance and happiness in their careers. Theo Davies, Head of Cloud Sales Enablement JAPAC, Google, says:

> 'The number one reason people leave is they don't feel they're making a difference. Either they are not recognised for making a difference, or they don't feel that the actual job that they do is making an impact or changing anything and their contribution is worthless.'

Radoslav Ivanov, International Sales Executive, Historical Park Bulgaria, agrees:

> 'People need praise and approval for their achievements. If you are working hard and you do not see anyone saying, "Hey, great job," that means

something is not right. We are human beings – everybody wants to be praised, everybody wants to be approved by the group. We are herd animals in a way.'

Why celebrate

Group celebration is powerful. Corbin McGuire, MD, NDM Recruitment, has a great analogy:

'The CrossFit phenomenon is a good example of this. What is CrossFit? Push-ups, sit-ups, pull-ups. Are those new? No. They have been around forever. Then how are they transforming bodies? They are getting people to do push-ups, sit-ups and pull-ups at record paces and at higher reps than people have ever done them before. How? Competition. Energy. Passion. They have created a culture and environment of energy. It is producing insane reps which is transforming bodies. People see the playbook works and buy in.'

Simon Ruddick, Chairman, Albourne Partners, highlights recognition as a need for the sales function:

'I think all the best salespeople are optimists and enthusiasts. Salespeople are also the most gullible people in the world because they live in an optimistic plane. I think, if you create an environment where they are loved, feel loved, then they tend to support each other.'

How to celebrate

Look for a leader who celebrates like Richard Humphrey did at Saatchi & Saatchi:

'I used to find parties very successful… Socials at business get-togethers, if you like. For instance, you congratulate a team within the company whenever you win something. Those little celebrations start to build a sense of belonging and shape the culture.'

Stuart Lotherington, Managing Director, SBR Consulting, appreciates an alternate form of recognition:

'I have been lucky enough to pretty much have an incentive trip every year for the last thirty years. We did very well as a company last year, so we took the entire team for a weekend away as a reward. I think that if you do not reward people for the success of the organisation, which is ultimately their success, then I think you will be in danger of eroding the relationship and the emotional bank account that you have got with them.'

KEY TAKEAWAY

Look for an organisation that offers a level of celebration appropriate for your level of performance. Even if it's small but frequent praise for the small wins, it's important to ensure you find an organisation that recognises sales.

Lesson 44: Check their sales focus and process

Make it sales-led

Stemming from leadership (lesson 50) and flowing down into the organisation is the sales focus of an organisation. Monica Hartman, Director, Gartner, says:

> '[With] the models that they talk about, sales is in the centre because the decisions that other business units make and the way that budgets are prioritised lean towards Gartner being a sales organisation. Having experience on the service side and on the product side, it's definitely true that the sales world is a priority over the others.'

Avi Wiesenberg, CRO and startup advisor, says:

> 'You can get companies with product-driven marketing strategies, or a sales-driven culture. I think there is a huge benefit in starting in a sales-driven organisation, because they are investing in their sales team. They understand that they will win or die as a company based on how good their sales execution is. That means they are investing in their sales team, as opposed to a company that is potentially only investing in the marketing or any investing in the product.'

This gels with my experience at P&G, a marketing-and product-focused organisation at the time, which meant the sales training was not as focused or complete as the sales-focused organisations I joined later.

Sales processes

It's important to test for the right level of sales process in an organisation before you join. Peter Kiddle, Chairman, Business Transfer Agent, says:

> 'I think it all goes wrong when you think you have got a good salesperson for whatever reason and then you throw them out in the field, you give them nothing else to help them, no support, no feedback, no coaching and then do not understand why they fail. It happens all the time, you see these firms failing. They are hiring and firing all the time and the churn is ridiculous. It costs a fortune and it does not get results.'

Brett Goodyear, Head of Sales EMEA, Challenger Inc, has this advice:

> 'When you're going to the interview process there's definitely questions you can ask: "What sales process do you run? What tools do you provide?" That's a double-edged question… If they tell you they're on their fifth system or fifth application and, "We've got an eight-stage sales process and we've got really strong checkpoints at the end," then you know they're quite an autocratic sales organisation

that's going to be really rigid around the sales process. If you hear someone say you're your own boss, that's great, that's very liberating, but what is the sales process? "Oh, no, we don't have one. Go and sell. We give you a number. We give you a car and some keys. Off you go." That's the other end of the extreme that should also send some alarm bells, because I think however good you are as a seller, you do need enablement.'

KEY TAKEAWAY

Having a sales-led organisation makes for less friction in your sales career and you can look to leadership (lesson 50) as a starting point. You need good guidance and structure that is well thought out and practised without being stifling. If you are looking to learn from great processes (lesson 70), you need them to already be in place.

Lesson 45: Make sure you can progress

Career progression considerations

The ability to progress at an appropriate pace within a company must be a key consideration. Felipe Poveda, Head of Sales EMEA, CreditSights, has this to say about his previous company:

'My earnings were obviously not maximised, but I was rewarded appropriately. I'm taking a larger pay rise by moving companies than if I moved internally again, and that probably shows that I was slightly underpaid. But it also gave me the ability to participate in something more like a journey; in something that gives you satisfaction on a multi-year basis. I was a small shareholder in that business, which felt like it was worth more than its monetary value or the monetary value of jumping around. I feel that if you find a good company, in my experience it's worth extending until its time rather than just moving for the sake of slightly better pay.'

Training

A big part of your progression within a company is the training that the company provides, and it should be increasingly possible to find it. Brett Goodyear, Head of Sales EMEA, Challenger Inc, says:

'CSO Insights, which is a research business, shared some data that showed that something like 50% of companies over $500m have a sales enablement function after 2016. Before 2016, it was something like 10% to 15%. That's massive growth in sales enablement, which is helping to professionalise the frontline and the sales processes and all the tools that people have.'

Theo Davies, Head of Cloud Sales Enablement JAPAC, Google, says:

> 'I love this question that managers sometimes have, "Well, what if I invest in training and they leave?" The other question to that is, "Well, what if you don't invest in them and they stay?" So obviously, when you go to training, you're really sharpening the sword. That compounds over time because as people get better from training, they also teach their peers on the ground, in the trenches and in the field. It's changing culture. That is one of the hardest things to address in any organisation, especially a large one.'

KEY TAKEAWAY

If you're a young, aspiring salesperson, ensure that you have access to training and progress opportunities so you can learn and be challenged. Yet the same applies if you're an older salesperson – progress and training is a continual process.

Lesson 46: Understand the interaction with other functions

Benefits of aligning

Whether or not functions work together – regardless of company size and life stage – has a huge bearing on the effectiveness of the sales function. Ronald Sluiter, Global Director, Gartner, describes an ideal scenario:

> 'We're all about sales productivity and efficiency. The systems do all the internal reporting now. We measure things, but not too many – only four or five measurements should be discussed with your manager. Every stage is monitored efficiently. It can be very frustrating in other companies – time spent internally cannot be spent with your customers so that is less time spent on achieving your goals. I would not choose a company which has a lot of internal meetings and wastes my time. I do not have to sell internally, which is a big relief. In other companies, they spend 60% of their time internally getting all the processes, proposals, and pricing right. We do not have that, which is good.'

Aligning with marketing

As consumers and companies make an increasing amount of their buying decisions before engaging with suppliers (up to 57%, lesson 14), sales' engagement with marketing to influence prospects in that initial stage is more important than ever.

Katrin Kiviselg, Partner, NorthStar Consulting, helps sales and marketing align in startups:

> 'They don't put the functions together and make them communicate, which is sometimes funny because the marketing person works on

lead generation, and the marketing message is completely different from the message that the salesperson is trying to close on.'

Brett Goodyear, Head of Sales EMEA, Challenger Inc, sees sales and marketing alignment as essential for a Challenger organisation (lesson 6). He says:

> 'I think one of the problems you find in a lot of companies is marketing is quite separate from frontline sales or from the business unit. You don't always have that luxury of getting them to help. What you're really after is the individual sellers not having to do the hard work for themselves every time. The sellers that fail are the ones that don't have the customer understanding and ability to build their own insights easily. The way that you make Challenger easier to learn is you build the insights for them, and that requires a cross-functional capability and effort.'

Aligning with product

Likewise, having a great product roadmap is key to successful sales. Carolin Berger, Regional Sales Manager, Outpost24, says:

> 'It is very easy to find an amazing product at a certain time and meet a certain customer need, but customers evolve and change and your product has to meet their evolving needs as well. You need really good

product management that has a vision and can drive that development.'

KEY TAKEAWAY

Ensuring marketing is giving you the right message, at the right time, with the right product and delivery in place are all key for sales. Check for coherency of message, clear competitive advantages and great customer or client feedback to ensure your own selling success, and look for an organisation that is aligned to reduce internal friction.

Lesson 47: Finding a compensation model that fits

Variability

As discussed in lesson 22, the more variability and risk you are willing to take, the greater the compensation. Thomas Haas, of a large SaaS (Software as a Service) company, recommends this approach for those with self-belief:

'You've got to be someone that believes that, not necessarily in one year, but you've got to believe that you as a person, within three years in the right organisation, are going to be successful; you're going to be a leader or a front runner. For me, I want the maximum opportunity in total, and those are the jobs that they cater for here: salary commitment is very low upfront, and you only earn loads of money in the scenario where the company makes loads of money. I like going into every year being like, "I might make £80,000 this year, I might make £300,000 this year; let's see what happens."'

The potential for equity as a form of variable income came up in several interviews, including with Simon Ruddick, Chairman, Albourne Partners:

'We don't do commission-based pay, but in its place, we use equity actively and aggressively. I think that I try to create, not a band of equals, but we use that as a metaphor for the true respect we feel for our fellow colleagues. That has been our alternate to commission-based sales and we just think it's the sincerest form of enlightenment. It's not about how I maximise my next pay cheque. I like to think of the multigenerational value of the equity that we hold.'

Achievable targets

Likewise, those targets must be achievable. Ronald Sluiter, Global Director, Gartner, shares his experience on unrealistic targets:

'I see this in software companies that try to recruit me... Every two weeks, I get a call. "You can earn an amazing OTE (on-target-earnings)." Wow! But then I ask them, "So how many people can achieve that kind of target?" and it becomes very quiet.'

KEY TAKEAWAY

Whether it be salary or equity, and based on modest or huge growth, ensure that the compensation model you choose works with your current lifestyle and life stage.

7
Lessons On People Considerations

'When I was interviewing for this company, sixteen years ago, I remember that I wanted to be wowed by the people I was talking to. If I was not blown away, I didn't want to work with them. What type of people was I going to be around? Because those are the people I am going to learn from and they'll have my little baby career in their hands.'
— Andrew Santos, CEO, Compass Group

Lesson 48: Choose your peers and collaborators

People you work with are key

In terms of what's most important in a job, Richard Humphreys, ex-CEO, Saatchi & Saatchi, says:

'It would be the other people on the team, I think, because it's a team business. You don't want politics

147

in the office if you can possibly help it. I think it's to have rapport with people. A team can be greater than the sum of its parts. Of course, you do need different talents. You need creative flare, of course, but you also need more. Sometimes it might be clear that they're looking for a certain type of person to make the team whole. Could that be you? Could you fit into that team and create more with these people with whom you can form a rapport?'

Sam Lewis, Partner, Albourne Partners, agrees:

'I think it always comes down to the people. One can achieve success in the short run, but if the people you're working with aren't good people, it really devalues the whole experience because you don't know if you're getting paid and treated properly and honestly. If it's a long-term journey, you have to wake up and work these people day in, day out, and that's a part of my job. For me, it begins and ends with people. Everything else is detail.'

Look for transparency and availability

Raf Tristao, Head of Strategic Accounts, HG Insights, says:

'Our vice presidents and directors are always willing to lend time. They can be busy with all their own things, but they set thirty minutes with you, and they're willing to give you their eyes and see where you're going wrong or come up with the game plan. That's leading by example. If you start taking your foot off the gas or missing numbers, then you feel like you're letting the team down not just yourself, and that's a big motivator for me. I don't want to let everyone else in the room who's working hard down by underperforming. Those are the key things I look for in colleagues: building that culture, being willing to lend you their time, being good at the job themselves, obviously and having that work ethic.'

Hang out with the best

Ensuring that colleagues, collaborators and team members are quality people was a constant theme. Radoslav Ivanov, International Sales Executive, Historical Park Bulgaria, has a requirement:

'I want them to have a goal. If they do not have a goal and they just join the team because they like me or someone else on the team, or they just like the idea but then do not put the effort in, I do not feel like it is a fair system.'

Dimitry Toukhcher, CEO, LGFG Fashion House, seeks out the best:

'In school, C-grade students will spend time with other C-grade students and A-grade students spend time with A-grade students. Sales is a reflection of life if you check your friends and who you are hanging out with. If you hang out with a bunch of losers, it is going to be really, really hard to be good at sales because your perception of the world is going to be reactive and you'll feel like a victim. If you are around winners, you know winners tend to have an attitude... That is very influential.'

KEY TAKEAWAY

Sales is a team business, so try and choose your company based on people who will influence you positively, and ensure that you spend time with the top performers that inspire you and make you better.

Lesson 49: Choosing your manager

Management style is crucial

In one of my earlier jobs, I was called into a room with my manager and a colleague. He proceeded to praise my colleague, who was producing good results after six months in the business, and to lambast my poor results after two months in the business. He went so far as to say, 'I produce better results than you, and it's not even my job to sell.' I felt awful, because of his harsh words, and because of what it revealed. Both his focus on bottom-line results (lesson 60 on the maths of sales) and his choice to have this comparative meeting confirmed that I had made a big mistake.

In my haste to get this job, I had overlooked that my manager wasn't the right person.

Jeremy Jacobs, The Sales Rainmaker®, has sound advice:

> 'If you can find a manager who offers to help people, who understands sales and understands life, and really takes an interest in you as an individual, that is ideal. You are not going to get that in a transactional place, ie, "You do this, here is your target, get on with it." You want a more transformational environment where people are allowed to grow and feel and can ask for help.'

Felipe Poveda, Head of Sales EMEA, CreditSights, says:

> 'I don't think you can work for someone that you don't admire at some level, professionally but also personally, for long. I don't think you can hate someone personally but admire them professionally. There's an element of admiration, feeling that you're going to learn something from them, because otherwise you won't want to stay in your role for long.'

Downsides and upsides

Working for a bad boss can have huge downsides. Connie Smith, Consultant, Whitten & Roy, describes her experience at a previous job:

'At first I was selling pretty poorly. I was selling really compulsively and really aggressively, because as a salesperson you are only ever performing at the level that your manager is. If they are harassing you for numbers, if they are in a survival state, that is exactly where you are going to be. If they have checked out mentally, their team will do the same. If you are furiously running after numbers, making mistakes, then that is what leads to burnout. My advice to my younger self who was in those unhealthy management relationships would be, "Get out now, just get another job," because the reality is that everyone needs sales people and there are loads of great sales jobs with great people and cultures.'

Conversely, a caring boss can have an enormous positive effect. Corbin McGuire, MD, NDM Recruitment, shares an experience:

'I remember I had a sales guy that was trying to make his first recruitment placement. When he did he was all excited. You could see him go, "My gosh, this works." And he had energy because he saw it work. A week later the client called me and said, "Hey, the guy that you placed left so we need our money back." I never told my sales guy because I knew that if I told him that he hadn't got the deal, he'd lose his energy. I paid him his bonus and congratulated him, and because he was so high on it he did exactly what he'd been told and it worked.

He worked harder because he had higher energy and he had three deals the next week.'

How to get a good manager

Thomas Haas, of a major SaaS business, has some sound advice:

'What I have asked in interviews in the past is, "OK, who will be managing me?" Then I'll ask to talk to that person directly. I'll say to them, "Can you give me an example of how you've developed someone where they were before, what you did and where it got them to?" That's a question that I asked my current manager.'

Theo Davies, Head of Cloud Sales Enablement JAPAC, Google, has a radical suggestion that has worked well for him:

'Go out and interview managers. When I went into real estate, my company got a shock. I walked into the agency and I said, "I'd like to speak to the top producing manager here please." I walked up to his desk and said, "Hi, my name is Theo. I'm considering your firm with a few others. Here are my credentials. I know I'm going be successful with this. I'd like to have a chat." Then I interviewed him, and I did that with the other three top houses in the country.'

KEY TAKEAWAY

You can't always interview your manager forensically, but ensure you screen your managers for quality – it's worth it. A good one can teach you a fantastic amount, and a bad one can inhibit your rise towards being exceptional.

Lesson 50: Company leadership is key

CEOs with sales experience

From a sales perspective, ideal company leaders are salespeople themselves. Luckily, this is becoming far more common (lesson 21). Stuart Lotherington, MD, SBR Consulting, explains why this is desirable:

> 'What I find in organisations that are led by financial individuals is that they really do not understand salespeople and are potentially at a risk of damaging the relationship. You need to have salespeople incentivised.'

Roger Philby, CEO, The Chemistry Group, admits:

> 'I think what my sales background has done is slightly skewed the emphasis towards sales in The Chemistry Group. I think that what me coming from sales means is that I am quite adamant

that everyone should understand the value of selling. Everyone should be selling.'

Toxic leadership

Toxic leadership can have a trickle-down effect. Peter Kiddle, Chairman, Business Transfer Agent, says:

'A toxic culture typically starts with either the owner or the managing director – whoever is in day-to-day direct control of that business. Sometimes I have gone into organisations where the owner would literally scream at people all day. You could hear him screaming at different members of staff and they would tremble when it was their turn to go into his office.'

Despite market-leading pay, the attrition rate at that company was apparently atrocious.

Look for a 'servant leader'

The recommendation from most interviewees was to look for transparent, supportive leaders: servant leaders. Richard Kiddle, Director, Titanbay, says:

'Where I am at right now, we have direct access to the founder himself. He sits in on meetings, comes to drinks in the evening, and they have made it very clear that we can have frank conversations at any moment in time. I have actually never been in a room like it. The questions we were asking were not to a multimillion hedge fund owner. They were basically like what you ask your parents.'

Jason Dial, Chairman, LGFG Fashion House, epitomises this type of leader:

'Yes, my title is president of LGFG, but I work for every employee there. My job is to make sure they know exactly what they have to do; to believe that they can do it; to hold up a picture of them that is bigger than their current picture and constantly remind them that I will see them that way until their actual picture is either that size or larger than what I am holding up.'

KEY TAKEAWAY

Look to the leadership for transparency, availability and goal setting. For you to have an exceptional career, your leadership needs to be exceptional.

Lesson 51: Choose your mentors

Importance of mentors

Having a mentor is key, and our interviewees were quick to tell me why. As Jeremy Jacobs, The Sales Rainmaker®, explains:

'Why should people have a mentor? Because if you are constantly in a situation where you are working with one person, like a sales manager, they may not have the time to mentor you. They will coach you and take you through various techniques; whereas a mentor would take on a different role, a more long-term role, and look at your outside interests. A mentor would look at your life as a whole, not just the sales job you are in at the moment.'

Sam Lewis, Partner, Albourne Partners, agrees:

'Number one, find a good coach. The best training, the best guidance you can ever have is from somebody who's done it before. If you could find a mentor or a coach, that's terrific. If you can find any means to test drive the car, nothing beats that. You can sit in a simulator all day long, but until you get out on the road or in the air, it's a different feel, and that makes everything come alive. Mentoring and coaching are supremely important.'

Manny Gonzalez, Financial Advisor, Raymond James, has a great mentor example:

'I give all props to my mentor, because when I first started in my career, he sat me down… When I was talking to my mentor, he said, "Manny, the first five years are extremely difficult. They're very, very hard. You're going to want to stop, but I promise you, you push through it; it's the most rewarding part." It was those words of wisdom from a mentor that really got me through those first years.'

How to get a mentor

Mentors are definitely out there and willing – the challenge is to find them. Hans Keijmel, Strategic Account Director, Bloomreach, notes:

> 'Then, of course, the question is, "How do you find a good coach?" I think that you have to look hard for people who are really interested in what you want to do, what you want to achieve, and how you want to achieve it.'

Simon Ruddick, Chairman, Albourne Partners, shares the joy of being a mentor:

> 'Almost by definition, the joy of mentoring is something that comes at a later stage, as it is hard to do that from the start. So yes, I'd say that's the greatest joy during the latter years or twilight years.'

Amanda Derham, Director, The Agile Director, helps links startups and mentors all the time:

> 'A lot of people, particularly fifty-five and over are very interested in helping. They want to transfer these skills. They want to help and they often say they do not need money to help. The validation of their own ideas is often enough, and they are delighted to support them. There is a lot of goodwill out there. It is a matter of connecting with those people.'

KEY TAKEAWAY

Having someone on board for your long-term career planning and actively interested in you is invaluable. Paid or unpaid (see lesson 69), find a way to get people who have done it well themselves to increase your chances of an exceptional career.

Lesson 52: Influence your territory, choose your customers

Laying the groundwork for good territory

You won't always get to immediately choose your sales territory, but you can influence and plan for the future. Not all sales territories are created equal, and exceptional salespeople will acquire (and create) the best territories over time.

Felipe Poveda, Head of Sales EMEA, CreditSights, has this advice:

'In terms of getting a good territory, it's almost impossible to negotiate that upon entry because you have very little leverage and your primary goal is to get the role. Once you are more established in an organisation, in terms of improving the territory, it can then be negotiated.'

Jon Begg, Head of Trade Marketing, RB, says:

> 'If you're on 20% growth channels, you never get
> a target of 30% to 40% so you've always got a real
> opportunity to over-deliver. Conversely, if you're
> working on one of the channels which is flat or
> even slower... your target is always still asking
> for growth. That makes it much harder to deliver
> a plan.'

Your customers

You should also aim for territory where you want to
work and can create longstanding relationships with
customers of your choice. Hugo Barclay, Owner, Art-
Thou, has designed his career with this in mind:

> 'I can choose who should buy from me and who I
> want to work with long-term. In a larger organisa-
> tion, you basically lose the autonomy to say, "Yes, I
> think you are the right type of person for this busi-
> ness," and you just kind of say yes to everybody.
> And that is fine, but it goes away from the mission
> and the element of quality that I prefer.'

Richard Kiddle, Director, Titanbay, shares an extreme
result of how choosing a territory that suited him led
to being hired by one of his own customers:

> 'I got a call from a guy that I used to work with
> regarding an exciting opportunity. I had previ-
> ously pitched to him quite a few times. He said,

"You know, I noted that you had one of the best sales processes that I have ever come across... I would like to meet you and run an idea by you. Please do not turn me down." When we met for coffee, he explained the concept [and] how he wanted the culture to be... I agreed with him that we would go for it.'

KEY TAKEAWAY

Plan for the territory you want to have, earn the right to that territory, and ask for the business (lesson 67) when the time comes. The ability to have long-term relationships in a territory that suits you, your personality type and your ambitions is invaluable.

8
Lessons On Getting Your Foot In The Door

'I remember one case of one of the investment banks, back in the big, bad old days when entire teams moved banks willy-nilly. The whole commodities desk moved to another bank and the junior team member who used to run the tickets up and downstairs was the only one left. The manager took the view that, "He knows roughly what's going on," so he became head of the desk. That was a stopgap – they hired other people, but that was his massive leg-up to become a sales trader and then earn a gazillion dollars. It's all about breaking down barriers and being present and being a good person.'
— Sam Lewis, Partner, Albourne Partners

Lesson 53: Do your research for interviews

Do your research

You can't just walk into an interview, at least until later in your career, and expect to get the job. Likewise, you can't be sure the job is right for you without doing your research. Always remember: any interview process is a two-way street, and your research will underpin mutual success.

Monica Hartman, Director, Gartner, shares her approach to company research:

> 'You're not going to see things unless you start to talk to people in the organisation or the recruiter or the hiring manager. It's not necessarily directly asking, "What traits are you looking for?" because they aren't just going to give you that upfront, but asking questions like, "What are some of the traits that your best salespeople have? What about those who aren't as successful? Where do you feel they have a gap?" This allows you to back into the traits they are looking for without explicitly asking.'

Manny Gonzalez, Financial Advisor, Raymond James, says:

> 'Before I did this, I called people that I personally knew that were already financial advisors and I'd say, "Hey, how do you like what you do? What do you hate about it? What sucks? What's the most rewarding?" For me, it's a pretty serious deal, it's my life, so I wanted to interview as many people that I could to have a good idea of what I was getting myself into.'

Tailor your approach

One of the more basic ways you can display that you've done your research is to send a high-end cover letter. Lauri Kinkar, CEO, Messente Communications, says:

> 'Your CV might be somewhat interesting but this is just a list of chronological events. I always look at whether the person wants to work for us or just wants a job. Cover letters are important to me. You have to explain whether you are intrigued by the company. I see people writing cover letters that already start to go into their train of thought on what the company should do next. It's amazing how many cover letters (more than two-thirds of what I get) are about wanting a job but not related to the company at all. We all want a job, but it doesn't really explain why you would want to take them up on it.'

Really prep for success

If you've decided you want a job, really go for it in the interview prep. Rich Kiddle, Director, Titanbay, remembers his most important interviews:

> 'I would revise for hours. Honestly – if I had a mock pitch 8am in the morning on say, Tuesday, I would be revising for it from Friday and making sure I knew everything inside out. I would get my

dad on the phone asking very difficult questions. When I would go into the interview, I had already been asked those questions and had answers for them, even if they were outside the box questions. I do not think there is any other way to get it right apart from really hard work and practice.'

I completely agree with Richard's view – when I made the most challenging career switch of my life (from tangible products with P&G to strategic financial news in Debtwire), I rehearsed my product pitch for the interview over thirty times. It was word perfect to the point that the interviewers mentioned it was the best they'd seen. I believe that changed their view of me from a peripheral candidate with little relevant experience to a frontrunner for a very competitive job.

KEY TAKEAWAY

Getting your foot in the door depends on how much you really want the job. If you really want it, then there's no excuse for not tailoring your cover letter, doing your research and then practising your interview until you can't fail.

Lesson 54: Shadow or do initial roles

Importance of shadowing

Put simply, there is no better way to understand if a job is for you than to do it for a day. Manny Gonzalez, Financial Advisor, Raymond James, gives this advice to jobseekers:

> 'I would ask my mom and dad, "Who's your financial advisor?" Then I'd just go shadow that person. "Hey, I want to do what you do. Can I shadow you for a day, or half a day?" If their parents don't have a financial advisor, then I would go to the most successful person in the community and say, "Hey, who's your financial advisor? I want to talk to them." That's where I would start. Shadowing, and connecting with people.'

If you're nervous asking to shadow someone for a day, keep in mind that several organisational leaders I spoke to actually require it. Robin Mukherjee, MD, 2Circles Consulting, says:

> 'I have every single person that I interview come over in person. I have them come in… and spend a paid day in the business. It may seem like a lot, but they spend at least a day, maybe a day and a half, in the business and I watch them quite closely with members in the team. I give them a bunch of

numbers to call and I watch how they respond to that.'

Thesea Sproul, Sales Leader, Tom James, explains the company's interview process:

'They'd come ride in the field for a day with me. That way, we get to know each other, but also, they get to see literally what we do every day and who we're seeing and how we're selling the product. It's very hands-on the way we interview.'

Shadowing helps you

While not sales-related, my choice to shadow for a couple of weeks rather than jump into a career path really paid dividends. I was convinced at sixteen that I wanted to be a lawyer, liking the idea of wearing suits and getting in high-end arguments (and not realising both could readily be done in sales). My uncle was a partner in a law firm so I went to work for him for two weeks. I'm so glad I did – most people there were between neutral and borderline miserable, living either for the weekends or their hobbies outside of work. By the time the two weeks were up, my aspirations to be a lawyer were long gone.

KEY TAKEAWAY

Find a way to shadow someone exceptional. You'll network, gain early respect, and learn what the job is really like.

Lesson 55: Networking into a job

Get in somehow, some way

There's no better and easier way to get hired than by expanding or leveraging your network. Even if you don't start with many connections, you can create them during your job hunt. Phil Low, Growth Lead, Revolut, has this recommendation:

'Remember: be forward. Don't be shy. Go through the websites, through LinkedIn, find people, message them. That is so important. Otherwise, you won't be displaying the networking and approaching skills that would make you good at a sales job.'

Rich Kiddle, Director, Titan Bay, was successful at getting a high-end job through a recruiter even when he had been refused due to his educational background:

'I asked one of my friends who has a background in banking to ring up the same recruitment company and say, "I am looking for a job in private equity fundraising," and guess what? They had roles. So, I called the recruitment company back and said, "I think you are completely wrong. You are making the industry even more elitist around education than it already is." He said, "OK. Let's have a chat about it."'

Leverage your network

Your existing network is the most powerful tool to get you hired. Connie Smith, Consultant, Whitten & Roy, is an expert networker:

'I am seen as, and get used as, a resource… Being a good networker means that I definitely earn more money because of the people that I've been able to get in front of. It opens up a lot of sales opportunities and employment opportunities where a company will put me forward because of the opportunities I can open up for them. I get approached at networking events by people wanting to hire me.'

A long list of interviewees got their current role through former workmates. Hans Keijmel, Strategic Account Director, Bloomreach, is one example:

'I was just painting my house, thinking about my next step, and then my former boss said, "Well, these guys are looking for a sales manager," and I said, "OK, what are we selling?"'

Exceptional stories

If you're always looking for a way to expand your network, opportunities will present themselves. Will Ferrand, Global Director, Refinitiv, says:

> 'One of the guys on the graduate scheme last year got into this because he sold a manager a car. The guy was really impressed with him and he said, "I'd quite like to work in the city." They got chatting and the manager... hired him.'

Chris Soprano, advisor, BondChain, recalls an amazing story about people going above and beyond to get into financial sales:

> 'One guy used to call this company every day but they hung up on him. One day, the phone was ringing around 5:30pm, when he knew the hiring manager was always at his desk. The manager picks up the phone for once and the guy says, "Hi, I want to work on your desk." The manager responds, "I'm going to be at this bar in half an hour. If you're there in a full suit, I'll give you an interview."... Long story short, the manager hired him and he had an incredibly successful career as a broker... The reason I bring that up is that you don't need to know anybody. You can persevere. You can call people.'

KEY TAKEAWAY

You probably know someone who can get you an amazing job, and if not, with perseverance you can find them. Get networking, and get hired.

Lesson 56: Treat your interviews like a sales process

Sell yourself through the process

As a hiring manager myself, I get frustrated when people don't do all the same things they would do in a normal sales process. If you're not doing it now, why would I trust you to build rapport, ask great questions, prompt for answers, close the business and follow up promptly with clients in the future?

Phil Low, Growth Lead, Revolut, says:

> 'You have to sell yourself if you're going to go for a sales organisation role. That's so critical because, at the end of the day, you are the product. People aren't listening to you verbalising a specification sheet, they're listening to you as a person.'

Andrew Santos, CEO Compass Group, expects candidates to be as available and coachable during the interview process as they need to be in the job:

'I try to give them many things to do. I am really trying to scare people away... because that tells me if they are coachable. Are they really into this? Everybody says they can work hard. If I go to a room and say, "Show of hands, who is lazy?" no one says, "Me." I have them call people. I have them list what their goals would be. I have them memorise things. I have them do a bunch of different kind of tests... If they are not willing to do those things then it is not good. For example, I just called this guy back today, to set up a final interview. I called him at our scheduled time and he goes, "Hey, I am so sorry. I am at the DMV. Can you call me back later?" and I was like, "Probably not." Right there, in my mind I am like, well, he is not into it, and that is OK.'

Brett Goodyear, Head of Sales EMEA, Challenger Inc, highlights a way to ensure you sell yourself well:

'Once, we had to make some redundancies, and someone was literally coming into the role as we made the redundancies. This guy ended up getting three offers in the space of a month, almost immediately. He was just smashing it with offers, because he cold-called sales leaders to pitch them his CV. And they were so impressed by the fact that he made the effort to do so, that he used his understanding of sales.'

Sell yourself on social media

Social media is a great way to sell yourself during the process. Theo Davies, Head of Cloud Sales Enablement JAPAC, Google, says:

> 'If someone has made it to the final round, I want to see those references on LinkedIn… As a hiring manager, I won't go and do ten reference calls but I might read every single one of those ten references… and come closer to a decision. If one or two of the reference calls weren't that good but they had ten great references on LinkedIn, that might be enough to sway me.'

Don't give up after the first 'no'

If you don't give up in sales after the first 'no,' it will service you well (lesson 12). It's the same during the interview process. Phil Burgess, Chief People Officer, C Space, says:

> 'I like it if someone is applying to be a salesperson and if I turn them down for an interview, they come back at me with another approach. I will give them the time of day and say, "OK, this person has a bit of a spark to them." I certainly interview people whom I have said "no" to, and they come back again, because I think that is what I would want you to do if you are selling to our clients.'

Brett Goodyear, Head of Sales EMEA, Challenger Inc, says:

'When I was a hiring manager and was most impressed with people, it's the ones that had the courage to, ever-so-slightly, bypass the traditional recruitment process. Once they know that you're the hiring manager, they make a direct outreach that's well-worded, shows intelligence, shows eagerness, doesn't pressure, but just does something to show that they are definitely interested and there's real intent. There's a real desire to show that they're proactive and assertive because that's exactly the skills that you want to share with a client. I've had HR managers come to me and say, "Hey. This person leapfrogged the process." I'm sorry, I want this guy or this girl in the process because that's exactly the skills that I'm after!'

KEY TAKEAWAY

Getting a new job that you really want can be a game-changer in an exceptional career, so be bold and innovative in your outreach and follow up during the hiring process.

Lesson 57: Extracurriculars can really help

The value of extracurriculars

Extracurriculars have the benefit of helping you develop skills that are more likely to assist you with getting your foot in the door. Ilias Varth, CEO, Owiwi, has run psychometrics for tens of thousands of recent graduates. He says:

> 'You might consider a degree a hard skill because there are things that you learn from it like business management and communications, but nowadays everyone has a degree or master's degree so it is very hard to differentiate and to stand out. With all the automation that is coming in, a lot of hard skills are not required or necessary anymore because we have software that does it for us, especially when we are referring to recent graduates. I think this is where soft skills really become relevant. The way that we see it, especially within the Millennial and graduate market, soft skills are the only key differentiators among that talent pool. Because of the fact that they are trainable, they are also a lot more attractive because you can "hire for attitude". Soft skills are the embodiment of that. Whether or not you are a team player is crucial in today's world. Whether, for example, you can carry yourself with integrity and have ethics is also becoming extremely important both for job seekers but also for employers.'

Lee McCroskey, speaker, trainer and coach, Southwestern Speakers, believes good presenting is a game-changer:

> 'If you can get up in front of a group and persuade them or influence them, then that gives you confidence. Also, a lot of people are doing consultative selling or group selling now, and if you go into a company and you have to present or demonstrate to a group of people, including senior leaders, I think it is a good skill to have. You just have to do it. That is part of my classes, no matter what class I am teaching. They have to get up in front of the class and do a presentation.'

I have personally found Toastmasters exceptionally helpful in developing soft skills,[11] but social media, involvement in charities and any organisational leadership position will potentially stand you in good stead to develop soft skills. You can find more ideas at www.exceptionalsalescareer.com/resources.

Exams

Being willing to study for profession-specific exams can also get you ahead. Rich Kiddle, Director, Titanbay, studied to gain access to the traditionally closed world of fundraising:

---

11 www.toastmasters.org

'I got to the point where they liked me, but they were unsure of my background. I had to negotiate with them and say that in order to prove myself, I would take the exams before I began. So, I did that… which has been a blessing really because… I got the job that I am currently in.'

Going above and beyond

There are things you can do in preparation for interview which will really amplify your messaging and chances of success. Theo Davies, Head of Cloud Sales Enablement JAPAC, Google, shares two examples that wowed him:

'Outside of the job application and the interview, this individual connected with me on social media. He had been putting out social content, specifically videos of him delivering sales training sessions. It was a well put together, well thought out, and well delivered programme, which showed so much more than I would ever have gotten from an interview… Another candidate who I hired attached a one-minute introduction video with a very creative message as part of his application. [It was] personalised to me and the other manager that he knew he was going to be meeting. [These examples] showed their keenness for the job. It showed their credibility and it already showed, obviously, presenting potential.'

KEY TAKEAWAY

There are many options for extracurriculars and specialisms available that can help you get a job, and with an increasingly competitive market, you should try and do so. If that's not possible, try and get the edge by doing something that will make you stand out and improve your skills.

Lesson 58: Interview brilliantly

Authenticity

Once you get your dream interview, you need to practise (lesson 54) and nail it. Simon Ruddick, Chairman, Albourne Partners, values authenticity:

'My question is only, "What's your passion? What's your interest? Not work, or study or anything, but what is your interest?" There is almost no wrong answer to that, but there is one wrong answer, and that's when the person is trying to guess what will impress me… I want them to be excited, passionate and emotionally invested in something. The best answer I got when I asked what somebody's passion was, "I like cooking. I like baking and making cakes." So, I said, "Oh, that's kind of interesting – is it because of all the ingredients, the chemistry behind it, and that it's artisan and creative?"

The person replied, "No, I just like to feed people." You're in. That's it. You've got my vote.'

Phil Burgess, Chief People Office, C Space, says:

'Do I feel like I have interviewed them, or do I feel like they have interviewed me, and got me talking? Because that is what I am going to want them to do with the client. I think at the end of an interview, "It's about having chemistry with this person – have they asked me intelligent questions?" I hold salespeople to a higher standard than I might someone else in terms of whether they create a rapport with me at the start; not just using, "Ah, this is a nice room," or, "What is the weather today?" Have they shown some kind of genuine interest in me? For example, afterwards, have they followed up with a thank you note? I'm still amazed at how few people follow up with a thank you note. For a sales role, if someone does not follow up, I think that is crazy, because what would they then do with their clients? None of this feels like rocket science, but sales isn't rocket science. It is about building relationships. It is about transferring feeling; it is about understanding needs within an hour, which you can do with someone in an interview.'

Exceptional interview ideas

Caroline Berger, Regional Sales Director, Outpost24, shared an example of a candidate that showed an exceptional level of preparation during his interviews:

'There was a candidate who did an amazing slide-deck. First of all, what I really admired is that he actually created a slide-deck template with our company colours. A lot of them are basically black and white, which is fair enough. He downloaded our imagery from our website and created a company template. He then said, "OK, so I looked at your product. You have cloud security, and you have application security. For this product, I would approach these people. For that product, I would approach these people. I have already identified ten target accounts for each product area." That is where I thought, "OK. This is amazing."'

Leigh Cohen, Head of Sales EMEA, Sendbird, describes an idea he gave to a technical salesperson:

'It was a technical sales job for a sales engineer. I said, "Why don't you… create an app and present it in the interview. They have not asked you to do it, but you're just going to do it and show that you're not only passionate about it, you spent the time, you understand it, and here's something that you created and thought about."'

If all else fails, be sincere

If all else fails, you can use a 'try me and see' approach. If you believe in yourself, your conviction will come across. Greg James, financial advisor at a major US bank, says:

'Listen a lot. You have credibility when you listen instead of coming across as a typical salesperson. Then do what you say you're going to do. If you say you're going to call somebody back, do it. If you say you're going to get them a report, do it. How do you interview when you have no experience? You say, "Look, I've got twenty-five years of experience telling the truth, twenty-five years of... doing what I said I was going to do."'

Dimitry Toukhcher, CEO, LGFG Fashion House, says:

'The number one thing a person can tell me in an interview is: "Look, give me a shot and judge me on my performance." That's the opposite of focusing on asking about what base salary is guaranteed. The top people are making a lot more than the base, so that is where they should be aiming for.'

KEY TAKEAWAY

Being authentic and passionate throughout your interview process is crucial. If you can find an idea to make you stand out from the rest of the candidates, even better. Be sincere and show willingness to prove yourself, especially if you lack experience.

9
Lessons On Nailing The Basics

'I think that seeing younger sellers come into the profession and seeing it becoming professionalised is rewarding, because you realise that actually there's a lot of process, there's a lot of science behind it now, which I think was always undervalued. It's nice to see that starting to become recognised... It's not all about guys wanting to run around earning as much commission as possible. There are people that genuinely believe in sales as a career and becoming sales leaders.'

— Brett Goodyear, Head of Sales EMEA, Challenger Inc

Lesson 59: Nail your attitude

You're your attitude

'Your attitude determines your altitude' may be the world's cheesiest phrase (as is 'it's easy when it's cheesy') but I not-so-secretly love them both. Rich Halbrook, VP of Sales, McLeod Software, says:

'I believe you need to hire attitudes. I want to hire people who expect to win because I believe that people usually react to you the way you expect them to. I look for people who expect to win, people who are competitive; I think competitiveness is an attitude.'

JT Olsen, CEO, Both Hands, shares his biggest strength:

'It's probably my enthusiasm. If I'm not feeling enthusiastic, I'll make myself feel enthusiastic. I'm an alert, alive, friendly, cordial form of enthusiastic. You have to talk yourself into it sometimes, as you don't feel that way every day. But if you start telling yourself – and you coach yourself – enthusiasm can make a difference.'

Keep your attitude consistent

You need to find a way to keep your attitude consistent in sales. Corbin McGuire, MD, RNM Recruitment, shares this analogy:

'If I said to you, "Go paint ten strokes of paint on the wall… and a $50 bill will pop out," and if you do that ten times and a $50 bill pops out, tell me, what are you going to do next? Yes, you'll paint another ten times. Then another $50 bill pops out, and if it was that simple, what would you do – would you ever stop working? No, you wouldn't even go home. All the salespeople would stay up late. I mean, people wouldn't take holidays. If we said, "Hey, when you stop painting, the money stops," they'd almost kill themselves… It's not a work ethic issue, but if you go and paint ten times and you're told after you do that a $50 bill pops out and nothing happens, what will you do? You may try it again, and you may try it again, and after the fourth time, you take your ball and go home.'

Corbin highlights a key conundrum of sales. People battle to work in situations that are demotivating and when you don't succeed in sales, that can happen. You'll succeed on average, but you definitely won't succeed every time. So how do you keep your motivation high in those situations?

Factors you can control

Focusing on controlling what you can was a key theme throughout the interviews, and crucial among the short list of what was controllable was work ethics, work statistics, attitude and energy. Andrew Santos, CEO, Compass Group, says:

'Once you know where you want to go, figure out what your plan is to get there. Ideally, that plan is based on things you can control… It takes a lot of the anxiety out of, "Is this plan going to work?" When you design the plan based on actual history, actual data, then it is just a matter of sticking to it and following it because the result is mathematically proven. Now you just got to put gas in the car.'

When I sold door-to-door, most days were pretty awful, objectively. One concept we were introduced to – one I continue to this day – was the ritual of identifying three positives daily, regardless of how difficult they were to find. We would come up with things like, "Fifteen people waved back," and, "No one punched me today." We were grasping at straws, but it helped us to control our attitude in the face of constant failure.

KEY TAKEAWAY

If you focus on factors that you can control and keep your attitude and your energy high, you will be in a really strong position to become exceptional.

Lesson 60: Track your stats and understand the maths of sales

Downside of not knowing numbers

One incredibly reassuring thing about sales is that it can be broken down into the numbers, which will ensure success if you work hard enough. A "sales funnel" is the concept that, if you have enough inputs in your process (for example, prospects identified or approached), and you follow the necessary activities (such as meetings or proposals), a certain percentage of your inputs will become outputs (sales or revenue). You can see this in the figure below.

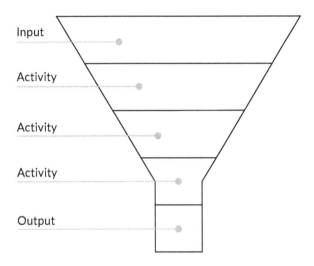

The sales funnel

Stuart Lotherington, MD, SBR Consulting, says:

'I am gobsmacked at the number of people that lack any concept of a sales funnel, conversion rates and activity metrics. I think the number one distraction from success for most salespeople is just not doing enough activity.'

Lars Tewes, Director, Clean Living International, explains what you should track:

'Between four and six key behaviours or activities, not just one or two. The most tracked activity is the proposal to win ratio; the conversion rate. Others end up being asked to track so much that it just becomes too complex. Whatever they are selling, they should be looking at the four, five or six core activities that will have the biggest impact on their performance; the income-producing activity.'

These activities will be your sales 'funnel' and typically start with prospects identified, down to approaches, meetings held, proposals, conversion and revenue. You'll then start to identify the ratios between the different pipeline stages. This might sound basic to some individuals and organisations, but many organisations somehow don't nail this.

The risk of not hitting your activity metrics

Ryan Dowd, Business Development Manager, COMATCH, says:

'There is nothing worse than falling just short. You never want to be in a position where you look back and say, "I could have done something more," or, "If I had worked a little harder…" or, "I didn't exhaust all of the things I could have done to try and close that deal or get that one more meeting."'

Raf Tristao, Head of Strategic Accounts, HG Insights, reflects:

'I would say if I could go back, I think one important thing is never taking your foot off the gas and
always finding motivation on a daily basis. Break it
down by day, by the hour or even break it down by
client. What do you need to work on this specific
day? That's the game plan.'

Learning through repetition

The advantage of playing the numbers is that you
learn through the process. Corbin McGuire, MD,
RNM Recruiting, says:

'Everybody's got a number on their jersey. My
number may be 81. So, once I get to 81 reps I've got
it. Other people may have a number on their jersey
that is 702. There are other guys that have 3,920,
but you're just trying to keep them energised until
they can hit that number. Once they hit their number, it's like that Thomas Edison quote: "I didn't
fail; I just I learned how not to do it a thousand
times." That's just what happens.'

Julio Hernandez, CEO, EnLight.Energy, has this
advice:

'The two big pillars that I would encourage someone to identify are trust and numbers. Trust and
numbers, everything comes back to that. How
many prospects can you get in front of? Then, how
good are you at helping that particular prospect

trust you? The person or the organisation that gets in front of the most people that trust them wins.'

KEY TAKEAWAY

Bringing sales back to the numbers is reassuring and gives you direction. Even if your organisation doesn't require it, I'd encourage you to identify your key success-driving activities, and measure yourself against both top-line and bottom-line metrics.

Lesson 61: Build rapport and trust

The advantage of rapport

Zander Fryer, CEO, High Impact Coaching, says:

'People buy from people they know, love and trust. I don't care how good your product or services are if somebody doesn't trust you. Not everybody, but 95% of people, won't buy from you if they don't know, love and trust you. There's that 5% that are just like, "Screw you, I'm going to buy it anyway just because I know I need it so bad," but 95% of people will not buy from you if they don't know, love and trust you.'

Richard Humphreys, ex-CEO, Saatchi & Saatchi, builds rapport though focusing on others:

'What's in it for them? That is, I think, the approach. People make buying decisions on irrational grounds sometimes. There is a human response factor in there – relationship, and likeability and things like that. Trust. The other thing is trust, of course, building a reputation for honesty, not over-selling the product.'

Rapport is crucial in winning an emotional decision that could go either way, and many interviewees were masters at establishing it. Interestingly, many interviewees didn't view it as a natural talent but rather something that can be practised and learned.

How to build rapport: listening and honesty

Rapport was generally considered to be a combined result of things as opposed to a moment where someone instantly likes you. Veronica Tribolati, Owner, HelloGuest, says:

'It's like a gift that they are giving you. Like it hits a hook. Take the hook. That's why it's really important to listen to them because they are telling you their story. Don't be a frozen salmon. Be human. You have a human in front of you, not just someone to milk money from.'

Phil Low, growth lead, Revolut, believes in a 'buying atmosphere' where the prospect feels truly comfortable:

'The sooner you can make it clear that the only outcome you really care about is getting to the bottom of their needs and whether you can help them or not, the better. You need to be engaging with people and to be able to really dig into their needs, and be honest as to whether you can help or not.'

KEY TAKEAWAY

While factors commonly discussed as the best ways to build rapport did include asking great questions (lesson 71) and using neurolinguistic programming (lesson 98), it appears that being human, providing comfort and being service-minded trumps all.

Lesson 62: Pitch brilliantly

Importance of elevator pitch

All salespeople need to pitch, so you might as well do it brilliantly. Nazia Khan, Business Development Manager, Outform, has this advice:

'Don't be afraid of job titles. You can run conversations at any level as long as you keep things really simple, clear and direct and you know what you are selling. You just have to be really clear before you get into the real game, and if you get a thirty-second elevated pitch down to a

T you will be successful, assuming there is a need for your product or service. Get your elevator pitch to the point where you could just wheel it off in your sleep.'

Lauri Kinkar, CEO, Messente Communications, says:

'I have flunked so many elevator pitches myself. I think that at the beginning of any conversation, especially if it is a cold conversation, it is super important to understand that you have a very limited time to pitch. For the cold approach, I get a lot of emails and I respond to very few of them. When you have a clear understanding of what you want, you are more inclined towards a good elevator pitch and developing it over time.'

Sales talk as key

Pitching doesn't require personal intervention – the tools to standardise your pitch should ideally be given to you by your organisation. Andrew Santos, CEO, Compass Group, says:

'They [salespeople] have to completely buy in to the system… I see a few people fail because they want to do it their own way, use their own words, which is not going to work out usually – especially when they are new. Not that we don't encourage people to be creative and develop things, but early on what they need is a really good sales talk.'

Richard Humphreys, ex-CEO, Saatchi & Saatchi, says:

> 'I always insisted that whenever we sold to new clients we produced a one-page executive summary that really captured everything that we were trying to get across. The other stuff you can stick in an appendix. They can read it if they want to, or they can get to what they need to know and then check it out. But you want the proposition simple and easy to access.'

Adapt your pitch

Having a memorised pitch should allow creativity and tailoring rather than preventing it. Nick Beresford, CEO, Enertor, has a horror story to share:

> 'We'd spent eight years on the presentation and got it down. It was all done right, all well researched; it was a spot-on presentation. I got there, and it was the main commercial director and one of the buyers, and I threw myself into the pitch. I went into all the data and all the insights. I thought, "Yeah." When I got to the end of it, they both said, "No, no, no, no, no," and kicked me out. It was a classic case of just going in and not asking any questions, not really understanding what they wanted. What I thought they wanted, they didn't – they were in a completely different zone. That's an example where I definitely got one wrong.'

Tailoring your presentation sufficiently, however, can make unlikely sales possible. Carolin Berger, Regional Sales Manager, Outpost24, shares the type of questions she asks to prove the superiority of the reports her company sells:

> 'They were comparing the quality of our reporting, so I asked them, "The data you see in our report, is it clear? Is it structured? Can you work with it?" And they said, "Yes." "In the other report, is it clear? Is it structured? Can you work with it?" And they said, "No, it is very confusing." So then I recommended, "Choose a product that enables you to do the job that you need to do. You need to have the information to take action. If our report gives you actionable insights, great. If the other does not, too bad." They totally bought into that and signed the contract the day after.'

KEY TAKEAWAY

Ultimately, you need both a memorised, word-perfect pitch and the ability to adapt it. Use your rehearsed pitch as a springboard for commercial creativity (lesson 93).

Lesson 63: Developing discipline

Discipline of prospecting process

Statistically, more than 40% of salespeople find prospecting the hardest part of their job and so spend less time on it than they should.[12] Mike Turner, MD, You-Become, shares his opinion:

> 'Interestingly, the one skill that's inevitably avoided most but which is the most important is prospecting. It is the one which is given the least time but actually the one which keeps a healthy pipeline of business. Someone needs to discipline [salespeople] in the organisation to invest enough time in their prospecting, because basically, if you've got a bulging pipeline, however bad a salesperson you are in terms of skills, you'll have enough in your pipeline to see you through. Prospecting, of all the skills of being a salesperson, is the one I would get a new salesperson to focus on.'

Jeremy Jacobs, The Sales Rainmaker®, says:

> 'The biggest reason why people failed in sales in the businesses I was involved in was probably lack of prospecting. It is almost absurd. You must not stop, because day in, day out, it is a relentless search. I think that is the word of this

---

12   A Frost '75 key sales statistics that'll help you sell smarter in 2020', (HubSpot, updated 20 December 2019), https://blog.hubspot.com/sales/sales-statistics, accessed 30 September 2020

interview – "relentless". A relentless search for new customers.'

John Willis, Director, 2Circles Communications, agrees:

'A common assumption would be that a salesperson needs to be naturally capable when it comes to their personal situations, but what's more important is the ability to apply a process and stick to that process whether you feel like it or not. Personality only gets you so far. The reality is that character wins over personality sooner or later. Character is extremely important in sales because it's all about not only doing things right, but also doing the right thing and being absolutely committed to the activities that it takes you to get to where you need to go.'

Discipline of activity

Radoslav Ivanov, International Sales Executive, Historical Park Bulgaria, says:

'It is basically the same with the gym. In the gym, it is easy for the first ten reps. When you get to eleven and twelve, it starts getting really hard. Basically, sales is the reverse of the gym. It is hard in the first couple of repetitions but then it starts getting easy because you go into that flow mode where you do not care anymore if they reject you, and you start constantly improving.'

Josef Dvorak, Country Manager, SBR Consulting, shares this insight:

'A great example of how to distinguish between average and professional salespeople is how are they able to navigate the little inner voice? I have my call list here at my right hand, and every time I look at it, my brain automatically tends to come up with an excuse as to why I shouldn't call now. Just then, I heard myself going, "Well, you know, you have this interview with Jamie in half an hour. Why don't you leave it for later?" The best don't do that.' (Josef made his calls and booked an appointment before he spoke to me.)

Discipline of thought

Discipline of thought is also key. Lee McCroskey, speaker, trainer and coach, Southwestern Speakers, says:

'I think if you really boil things down to what causes salespeople to win or not, it is what goes on in their mind. How do you control your thinking? There are two categories of thoughts as you are working: useful thoughts and useless thoughts. When I would ask a question like, "Why can I not work today?" my brain would always give me an answer. It was probably not true, but it would say, "Because you are lazy and not very good at this and you should probably quit." But useful thoughts are useful thoughts. For example, when I was first learning the trade, someone said, "Five years from now, something about today is going to make me a better person." If people can control what they think about, they will win big.'

Theo Davies, Head of Sales Enablement JAPAC, Google, draws on timeless wisdom:

'The first point is the focus and discipline. It's the old wisdom of Lao Tzu, [founder of Taoism]: Beware your thoughts as they become words. Beware your words as they become actions. Beware your actions as they become habits. Beware your habits as they become your character and your destiny. Where your thoughts are, your actions go, they become habits and they become who you are.'

KEY TAKEAWAY

If you can combine discipline of focus, process, activity, thoughts, word and deed, you will be in full control of your destiny.

Lesson 64: Trusting the process

Don't do things too quickly

The biggest recommendation of our interviewees was to look at your career through a long-term lens. Ultimately, you need to trust the process, especially in longer sales cycles (lesson 30). Ryan Dowd, Business Development Manager, COMATCH, has this advice:

> 'Just put your head down and crank. It is a grind. It is like running a marathon. You are not just trying to sprint from deal to deal, it is about establishing a consistent cadence. I aspire to have a sales pipeline that is metronomic; that I am consistent with meetings, deals and revenue, because that is when you get into a regular cadence. That is when sales can be even more rewarding, when you know you are set up to be consistent this quarter and next quarter. Then those sprints, that 100-metre or 200-metre sprint, those are the extra deals that you can chase on top of your target; the icing on the cake. Ultimately, you want to run the marathon.'

Ronald Sluiter, Global Director, Gartner, has this advice about timelines:

> 'You agree to set a certain date with the prospect. "It's June right now, would it be achievable and if everything goes well, do we have a decision by August?" You need to pinpoint a destination and time in their mind so that it is not an endless sales

cycle. There are investments of time on both sides, then at a certain point, they need to make a decision.'

This agreement tends to work (and rule out prospects that are not serious) and gives you the right to drive urgency.

Full belief

If you believe in the process, then the magic can happen quickly. Howard Paine, Regional Sales Manager, Zscaler, says:

'Surprisingly, my first end-to-end sales call ended up pulling through. It was a difficult one in terms of complexity, but I thought, "This is going to be my gold standard." I was going to do everything exactly as it should be, whether I felt it was worth the effort on some points or not. It took a lot of feedback sessions. I wasn't entirely sure in the outcome but trusted the process, trusted in the team and it went awesomely. We did all the right things at the right time; it wasn't any sort of magical knowledge or that I suddenly got lucky. I followed the process and just stuck with it in a logical manner and got advice when I needed it. It was as good of a high as you can get.'

Chris Soprano, advisor, BondChain, says:

'In the broking world, before the screens came in, we had a notepad. In the morning the notepad was empty – no price, nothing. I would sit there and say, "How the hell are we going to make money today?" Then we got on the phones and we started shouting to our customers, "Hey, what can we do today?" You got a price where you wanted to buy something or where you wanted to sell something, and at the end of the day, your blotter was completely full.'

Established processes

As you'll see in lesson 70, you should endeavour to understand great processes where they exist. Charles Talbot, MD, Pinpoint Recruitment, says:

'When you're a young sales guy, you don't realise how structure and sales process has been refined and improved and formalised over the years... Try to find a business where there's a lot of structure, so as a junior sales person you can concentrate on what you're selling rather than how you're doing it.'

KEY TAKEAWAY

If you can understand and implement great processes, you can avoid having to re-do great work that's already been done by 'standing on the shoulders of giants'. Believe and follow the process, and be humble enough to learn it well.

Lesson 65: Adapt your communication style

Change your style to make people comfortable

Lee McCroskey, speaker, trainer and coach, South-western Speakers, says:

> 'My big problem when I first started was that I thought everyone saw the world through my glasses. "I like to be sold this way, so I think everybody should…" Well, the fact is that 75% of the world did not see the world the way I did. Selling to people the way they want to be sold to is mission-critical. Discovering who you are dealing with, what their needs are and then orientating your whole presentation and delivery around their style is key.'

Peter Kiddle, Chairman, Business Transfer Agent, says:

> 'If you are really clever – and this is where I think selling is an art – when you go in to meet a customer, you are neither an introvert nor an extrovert initially. You are neither the expert nor the mouthy salesperson, but you ask a few questions, sit back, weigh up the individual and then mirror the style of that individual.'

Adapting to help people buy

Brett Goodyear, Head of Sales EMEA, Challenger Inc, says:

'Asking what personality is good for sales is like asking, "What's the right personality to be a buyer?" They come in all shapes and sizes. You can say there are some that are more successful than others. I've seen introverted people, quite analytical people, become drivers in terms of their communication style once they're leaders because that's the responsibility they assume... I think you can learn communication styles that can help you overcome any personality limitation you may feel.'

KEY TAKEAWAY

Communication styles can be learned, and by mirroring body language, voice volume and tone you can make people feel more comfortable and ready to buy from you.

Lesson 66: Know and sell value

Have product belief

Some of the interviewees were brimming with conviction in this regard. Simon Ruddick, Chairman, Albourne Partners, says:

'Every meeting I go into with Albourne, I think there are two outcomes – either they become a client, or they didn't really understand what I was saying. If they don't understand what I'm saying, it's because I should have said it clearer.'

Andrew Santos, CEO, Compass Group, says:

'I always ask people when I interview them, "Hey, if I came into your business and I showed you this insurance policy, would you buy it?" and if they don't say yes, then I won't hire them. If they do not believe in it enough or they don't own it themselves, they are not going to be very effective at helping other people see how I can help them.'

Jamie Badar, CEO, V2R, describes the difference between the features of a product and the value that it provides:

'It's about understanding the value of your product. If you're selling a drill, for example, you're not just selling the drill, but you're also selling the quality of the hole or how quickly you can drill holes. How they achieve that hole is neither here nor there. But if you know that your drill can produce that hole at a lower temperature, or in a quicker time, or going through fewer drill bits, whatever is important for them on the job – that's valuable.'

Recognise personal value

Product value is always important, but personal value to the individual will usually trump that. Will Ferrand, Global Director, Refinitiv, says:

> 'What is the incentive for the person to buy from you? Is it something that will make them look good in front of their boss? Is it something that will save them time... because this is part of the job they don't particularly like and they just want to get it over and done with? What is it that your customer is trying to solve?'

Dan Ingwell, Managing Partner, People Strategy Network, describes a scenario where his client had agreed that his solution would provide a £10m business value:

> 'The CEO said, "I'm not going to buy it." I was shocked, and said, "What do you mean? We've just both agreed that it's going to save you £10m off your budget. Of course you're going to buy it." He said, "No, I can't possibly do that because if I do, it's going to expose the weaknesses and the fact that I don't actually need as many people in my team... I'd have to sack some of them. Some of them are my friends, and I've worked with them for years. I'd rather lose £10m out of my organisation's and the taxpayer's budget and keep my mates in a job." 'I was absolutely amazed. That taught me that there's something called personal

value as well as business value. If you sell to business value, which everyone talks about and you absolutely have to do, it's not necessarily the only thing that matters.'

KEY TAKEAWAY

Tailor your sales presentation to get away from the features of the product (what it does) and towards the value (what it means). When you go a step further and highlight the value it brings to that person, the true urgency to buy manifests.

Lesson 67: Ask for the business and close

Asking for the business

I once went into a sales meeting with one of the premier experts in emerging market debt to meet three law firm partners specialising in the same area. I hardly said a word in the meeting – it was like watching a game of intellectual chess with both sides proudly displaying their knowledge. This went on for an hour and then the two sides agreed they should 'do this again sometime'. Not once did I ask them to subscribe to our news coverage of these markets – even right at the end. (My former company is still waiting for the signed contract for all the value we gave away that day – it must be lost in the mail...)

Anthony Charlton, Commercial Director, Gartner, says:

> 'Less than 50% of sales calls end in a request for the business. Not losing sight of that end objective is really important. Whether you are trying to close in that conversation or not, it is about setting it up to get to that close at some point, and how you get to a stage by the end of which you are laying the foundations for that close.'

Peter Kiddle, Chairman, Business Transfer Agent, shares a valuable lesson:

> 'It took a while to realise that I was a salesperson and not just somebody talking to customers. Those that do not understand how to close can have lots of meetings with lots of people and it can all be very friendly but they do not achieve anything. I was in that category – I was helpful and pleasant and yet lots of people walked away without buying. I would have wanted more help on closing, so that I could have brought in more sales earlier.'

Co-create proposals

Connie Smith, Consultant, Whitten & Roy, says:

> 'The biggest hurdle is making sure you don't fall into the trap of sending out proposals and then chasing them up. I have corrected this from years of selling badly... "Just checking in to see if you

have read the proposal..." You just chase up these proposals again and again. Now I never work on a proposal independently but build them with the client in real time – a collaborative proposal. We build it together on video call, sharing a screen. The final version is reviewed over a call. I make sure there is no situation where I send a proposal without running it through with the decision-makers.'

Close in the moment

Rick Halbrooks, Vice President Sales, McLeod Software, says:

'Somebody once told me that in every sales situation, a sale is made. I thought, "What in the world? I had a lot of sales where I didn't get a sale – what are you talking about?" Well, they say either you sell the prospect on doing business with you, or they sell you on why they're not going to do business with you.'

Rick also shared a lesson he learned from losing to a competitor:

'The competition said, "What's it going to take to get it done today?" They got creative and made the deal happen, and I didn't do that. [Now] I teach all my salespeople the same thing. Get it done today. Don't put it off until tomorrow or next week. If you do, there are more bad things that could happen than good things. The only good thing that can happen is that they do what they say they're going to do on Monday. Think of all the bad things that can happen.'

KEY TAKEAWAY

Too many deals are lost because the business is never asked for and concluded in the most efficient time window. Become exceptional at creating a mindset to ask for that sale and then closing it.

10
Lessons On Continual Learning

'From my observations this distinguishes the average salespeople from the top performers: whenever you speak to a top producer, he or she will always adopt a humble point of view and always be willing to work on his or her skills. The average salesperson usually says something like, "Well, you know, I've seen it all. I know it all." That's a fair indication if you're talking to an average or an exceptional salesperson.'
— Josef Dvorak, Country Manager, SBR Consulting

Lesson 68: Learning is a career strategy

Self-development gives you the edge

Excluding mandatory training (if there is any offered), the degree to which you develop yourself as a salesperson is optional. As Theo Davies, Head of Cloud Sales Enablement JAPAC, Google, points out:

'In my very first year of sales I learned from my manager that you will be exactly the same person you are five years from now other than the people that you meet and the books that you read. If you don't see any fundamental change that comes with the people that you work with, that you meet, that you hear, that you listen to, that you go to training with and that you see at conferences or seminars, then the other side is the books you read.'

Unfortunately, many salespeople spend little to no time on their self-development. There are exceptions, of course. Zander Fryer, CEO, High Impact Coaching, is one example:

'At this point we're bringing in great money but I still spend somewhere around $60k to $100k on my own coaching. People mentoring me, coaching me, going through programmes and things like that, so that I can continue to learn and continue to get better.'

The value of books

Sales books generally contain the curated wisdom of those who have successfully done it all before, but how many of these books do most aspiring salespeople read? Theo Davies, Head of Cloud Sales Enablement JAPAC, Google, says:

'I would say it's zero… If we took a snapshot of a hundred first-year rookie salespeople and we took the average number of books that they read in the first year, I bet it would be zero. It would take fifty people out of a hundred people to just read one book in a year to get past zero.'

Theo recognises the value of books as a means towards becoming exceptional:

'You can literally change your mind or your heart about something fundamental through a book… When I was asked to leave a gift for my successor, which is yet to be found, what I gave was an old Chinese antique mini treasure chest. Inside the chest, I wrote a list of the top ten books that he or she must read to get to the next level. If you want that list, you're going to have to go back and break that sales record to get it.'

Many learned salespeople readily credit their wisdom as being sourced from reading books. Jason Dial, Chairman, LGFG Fashion House, says:

'I am just a messenger. I take messages from books like Brian Tracy's *Goals!* and I introduce them to people. I am not the person that gets people to do things; I just introduce them to principles and then show them how to do it.'

Lauri Kinkar, CEO, Messente Communications, says:

'I know a few very good salespeople who absolutely dislike sales books. It's not a requirement to be a good salesperson, but I have almost never seen a bad salesperson who actively reads, which means that if you do… it's a sign that you are interested in your own craft. I think that gives you a high floor for success.'

KEY TAKEAWAY

Investing in your own learning is a simple way to gain a competitive advantage. Embrace it and accelerate your exceptionality.

Lesson 69: Learning about your industry and sales

Start humble and curious

Scott Roy, CEO, Whitten & Roy, says:

'Go into selling with an open mind and a willingness to learn. This goes back to what my early career taught me: work hard, study hard and be teachable. Go in with the willingness to learn your industry and about sales and things usually work out. I've been in sales and sales leadership for more than forty years and I'm still learning – and I'm supposed to be an expert at it.'

Ryan Dowd, Business Development Manager, COMATCH, says:

'I think one of the biggest differences is that intellectual curiosity piece. I think salespeople, the successful ones, do have a natural intellectual curiosity. It may not be their interest in politics, sports, travel and food – it may be that they have a narrow interest and go a little bit deeper instead of a mile wide and an inch deep. There is a certain volume that their mind needs to have filled. Nobody expects a salesperson to be the expert, there is a product guy for that, but being able to get up to speed very quickly on a new subject is key.'

The dilemma of learning

This dilemma of a narrow focus on an industry or a broader focus on exceptional sales and coachability is a pertinent one in terms of how you prioritise your learning. New industries take time to learn. Radoslav Ivanov, International Sales Executive, Historical Park Bulgaria, says:

'When I came to this new job, I had to throw away my ego. I had to throw away all my awards, all my accomplishments, and say, "OK. I am starting fresh. Now, I need to learn. I need to be quiet. I need to be coachable." You might be talented and experienced but if you are coachable and grateful for what is being provided to you, you are going to have a lot more success than if you act like a douche.'

Lauri Kinkar, CEO, Messente Communications, says:

> 'If it is something very complicated, it is better to know the industry. Someone I know is building a company a few blocks down the road. They deal with ticketing systems for transportation. This has so many complications that you are better off knowing a lot about that market. However, if it is a less complex sales cycle, then you are better off knowing more about sales techniques.'

KEY TAKEAWAY

The most essential thing, especially in your early career, is that you keep learning. Whether to focus on your industry or on sales techniques is a tough choice – the best option is to do both if you can.

Lesson 70: Shadow the best

Why shadow

One way to turbo-charge your learning is to shadow the very best. In addition to teaching you about the industry and ensuring it's right for you, every second with an exceptional salesperson can contribute to your exceptional enhancement.

Lars Tewes, Director, Clean Living International, says:

'The biggest piece of advice to an aspiring sales-person would be to spend as much time as they can shadowing successful, professional sales-people. Too many people who start out in sales go through a bit of early training and then are let loose to sell, rarely continuing their personal learning. There is not enough opportunity for young aspiring salespeople to learn from the good people out in the field. Personally, when I started out in sales, I was lucky enough to be able to shadow the top performers who gave me the confidence that I could do it as well.'

Steve Goknel, CEO, Your Edge Solutions, says: 'There is a lot that can be learned from other people. What you can learn from ten good people in two months will take you two years to learn yourself.'

Shadowing benefits

Aside from the learning that shadowing or being shad-owed can provide, it may also prevent you from costly mistakes. Jason Dial, Chairman, LGFG Fashion House, shares a shadowing experience he had as a mentor:

'I can remember following a young man – he was on one of his first sales calls. It was so bad… I went with them on the call and the guy was desperate to be successful. He was short, quick, and to the point and I had to jump in and help… because he wasn't listening. We walked out with a $50,000 clothing sale. He got full credit for it. It was a cool experience to see him go through that.'

Extreme shadowing

Some top performers have gone to extreme lengths to shadow those they wish to emulate. Theo Davies, Head of Cloud Sales Enablement JAPAC, Google, says this on the best thing about his career:

> 'I would say it was shadowing some of the best people, rubbing shoulders with them, but ultimately becoming friends with them and then becoming mentors. I remember one time, I spent $1,500 of my money to fly to Alaska to shadow the number one producing guy in the company.'

Zander Fryer, CEO, High Impact Coaching, explains:

> 'Understand that it's an investment, it's not a cost. I remember when I first started my business – I don't suggest anybody does this – but I basically spent all my savings and put myself into $20k worth of debt to learn everything that I could from all the best in the world. I knew the one resource that I could never get back was my time, so if I wanted to get really good at sales or marketing or business or communication, why would I try and spend the next five years figuring it out on my own?'

KEY TAKEAWAY

Putting yourself into excessive debt is extreme but it does underscore the importance of effective shadowing and mentoring. Request it, orchestrate it or seek out this accelerated route to success.

Lesson 71: Follow the best processes

Develop great process from the start

Brett Gartner, Head of Sales, EMEA Challenger Inc, shares this advice:

> 'I think that what I try and inject into young sellers now is, "Don't worry about the deal value. Don't worry about the dollar size. Don't worry about the commission check. That will come." You need some of those deals early on and you're going to be hooked. You're going to want to get better and better and better… rather than seeing it as a job of, "How well can I forecast and how long can I keep the manager off my back or when am I going to get this deal landed?" That stuff will just go, that stuff melts away if you can get your approach right and your real enjoyment from engaging a customer at their level.'

Believe in the process

Even those who start slowly can get there if they trust the process. Lee McCroskey, speaker, trainer and coach, Southwestern Speakers, tells the story of a young man who seemed completely unsuited for sales:

> 'He learned the material and he went to prospect after prospect, he had a slow start. Once he locked on to the system, he outsold everybody. He worked with me for seven years. As a university student he saved over $100,000 and travelled the world. He certainly changed. He can now look you in the eye, shake your hand and is confident. Ultimately, he had a lot of drive that you could not see.'

Specific processes

There are dozens of great processes to learn, but a few key processes that top organisations adopt are peer-to-peer learning, recording your sales meetings and role-playing as a form of practice.

Venetia Paske, Principal Consultant, SBR Consulting, has this to say about peer-to-peer learning:

> 'I literally just jumped off a call with two of my colleagues who are peers and we were doing a deal review using an internal tool that we have – a "playbook". It's not my deal, but even going through a colleague's deal and checking where

they are in terms of our sales cycle is helpful. We were analysing what has been done, what has not been done, and what questions you could ask. Our culture is founded on feedback, support and peer-to-peer coaching.'

Vlada Tusco, Partnerships Manager at an international media company, explains how she learns from recording her sales calls:

'I listen to them when I go on my daily walk… I will listen to some of it and I will quickly diagnose where I am in my level of engagement and enthusiasm and give myself one or two small things to focus on during the next call. I am not trying to overhaul my entire performance or pitch delivery, but just tweaking small things step by step makes me confident.'

Connie Smith, Consultant, Whitten & Roy, stresses the importance of role-playing:

'Role-playing is absolutely critical. It allows for them to make the mistakes, to feel all of that uncomfortable awkwardness that you do feel and just get it out of the way. It feels more like something they have practised. The second part of coaching somebody really well is you then ask them to do it, but you do not ask them to do everything from beginning to end, you break things down into small segments.'

KEY TAKEAWAY

These are just some examples of top processes –
others include great sales talk (lesson 64), tracking your
numbers (lesson 60), and exceptional prep (lesson 95).
Exceptional salespeople take pains to learn them and
use them whenever they can.

Lesson 72: Be curious and truly listen

Why be curious?

Curiosity is a career-long endeavour. As Lee McCroskey, speaker, trainer and coach, Southwestern Speakers, says, 'You've never arrived in selling. You never
go, "Well, I have maxed out. I am done. I am at the
pinnacle. Nothing more to learn here."'

Ronald Sluiter, Global Director, Gartner, agrees:

'Every step in the sales process, there is always
something to learn and perfect, and you will never
achieve that. The more you know, the more you
understand you do not know. You can sit down
and do your thing, or you can talk to people and
say, "Hey, I have a problem, is this how I solve it?"
or, "This is how I want to solve it, but what would
you do?" That way, you learn from the mistakes of
others. If you make your own mistakes then your
learning curve is very steep.'

Dan Ingwell, managing partner, People Strategy Network, shares this story about his son's combination of curiosity and listening:

> 'He used to listen to me coaching people in new business, role-playing with them in my attic office when he was in bed, supposedly sleeping. Then when he got into sales himself, the first thing he said was, "Remind me, what's that pacing and leading thing that you used to tell everyone about?"'

Truly listen

Listening is a highly viable sales skill, internally and externally. Nick Beresford, CEO, Enertor, says:

> 'You can achieve by almost saying nothing; just by listening and trying to find the problem that you can solve. It's very rarely about your product – it's much more about understanding. When people feel understood, there's a natural tendency to buy, so focus on developing the skill of listening.'

Jason Dial, Chairman, LGFG Fashion House, was genuinely uncomfortable being interviewed due to his natural listening ability:

> 'You just have to ask good questions and listen. A good salesperson never talks more than 20% of the conversation, which is why I'm not comfortable with you asking me questions and me doing all the talking. Listening is the most important skill

to cultivate. Listening to hear, listening to understand what the client or the prospect wants, and if you can help them. If you cannot help them, tell them. You have got to be able to listen. Everyone is going to tell you what they want; how they want it; and when they want it. If you do not listen, you are going to miss it.'

KEY TAKEAWAY

They told me to 'be a sponge' in my first sales training for door-to-door selling in Nashville Tennessee. Maintaining that sponginess throughout your career is tough and requires constant acknowledgement that you're never quite there – but the benefits of continual learning are worth it.

Lesson 73: Ask brilliant questions

The power of questioning

If listening is key to rapport (lesson 61), asking great questions is the key to maximising that listening productivity. Ollie Venn, Operations Director, Foxtons, looks back at his early career:

'I would have taken more opportunities... to ask more questions... Stop being a cocky little arrogant sales negotiator and just let people talk to you. If you listen, 80% of the time they will tell you everything… If you ask the right questions, you don't really have to do much talking. Just listen to people. They will tell you everything that you want to know.'

Will Ferrand, Global Director, Refinitiv, has this advice about asking questions:

'Try to understand the industry and… to understand their company – how their company operates; what are the products their company uses; how that all fits in; any issues they've had in the past… Just asking as many questions as possible really. I always think that there's no such thing as a stupid question. In some instances, when you deal with a buyer who feels they have all the power, asking the awkward questions puts them on the back foot – it shifts that balance and rebalances that power… Sometimes asking the awkward questions, especially with senior people, can get you a bit more respect from them. The worst thing they can do is refuse to answer it, in which case you're in the same situation you were if you didn't ask the question.'

Quality of questions

It's not just asking questions – having exceptional prep (lesson 95) allows you to ask insightful questions (which build rapport and credibility) and prompts better answers. Jamie Badar, CEO, V2R, says:

'Clarification is important because it shows them that they've been understood and people generally want to be understood. Mostly, people have this craving to be heard and be understood. "I've said something, but do you understand what I'm saying?" Feeding it back to them and paraphrasing it shows that you've actually digested the information and you really understand it. Asking an intelligent question on top of that means that you understand it and you're taking it to another level.'

Vlada Tusco, Partnerships Manager at an international media company, says:

'I think the quality of the questions you ask plays a really big role in the credibility that you earn and it plays a big role in the degree of value you provide... Open-ended, vague and generic questions are typically not incisive enough. If you know so much about the business that you can ask some really relevant questions that make them think, "You really get me," or, "How did you know that?" you can win them over easily.'

Great results

Asking the right questions can lead you to bigger sales. Peter Kiddle, Chairman, Business Transfer Agent, says:

'This particular call, I went in for a one-day time management course and came away with twenty-four different courses for five hundred people. The difference was that I am not an order-taker anymore. I am a consultative salesperson that found out what the real issues were at that business. Time management was not actually the issue at all. It was that none of those managers or leaders had had any training in the entire management and leadership arena. Once I realised what consultative selling means and what closing was all about, I picked up hundreds of thousands of pounds on each call.'

KEY TAKEAWAY

Asking the right questions opens doors and puts you in control of a sale. It also helps you access that valuable listening time which helps close the sale.

Lesson 74: Have many strings to your bow

Develop a portfolio career

The concept of a portfolio career is a simple but powerful one – to have multiple 'strings to your bow' that diversify your career portfolio. Rupa Datta, owner, Portfolio People, explains:

'We are not our jobs. Long-term you can get so caught up in living pay cheque to pay cheque; I've seen it happen throughout my career. Are any of us in positions where if the worst happened, [our future] would be within our control? Portfolio careers are a way to play your career game. Do you know where your next revenue will come from if you are let go from the position that you're in? If I were to get fired tomorrow, do I have things to do and people in my network that will open doors for me? Can I get another job through my network? That's why I'm probably more confident and comfortable than someone that is attached to just their job.'

Choosing your non-work portfolio

Wondering if you can do a new activity? Go ahead and do it. Zander Fryer, CEO, High Impact Coaching, gives this advice:

'Outside of the norm, I would say a couple of things that are phenomenal for all salespeople are things like Toastmasters and improvisation classes. Toastmasters and improv can really just keep you light-hearted and on your feet and comfortable in uncomfortable situations.'

Lee McCroskey, speaker, trainer and coach, Southwestern Speakers, recommends that you tailor your interests outside of work to your personality and your needs:

'My daughter needs to recharge. Her extracurricular activity is to be alone, get quiet and read, because she has been around people enough. She has poured herself into them and she needs to refill her cup. Other people, they need to go out to a networking event because they just get excited and enthusiastic being around other business professionals. They need to go connect and get wired that way. I think it is different for different people.'

KEY TAKEAWAY

It makes sense to have interests outside of work, to develop various skills and improve your network (lesson 80). Do things you enjoy, become good at them and set your increasingly well-rounded goals appropriately.

Lesson 75: Embrace and learn from the 'noes'

Why you should take 'no' well

Zander Fryer, CEO, High Impact Coaching, says:

'One of my mentors once told me when I first started my business (I was making nothing and he had a seven-figure business and was travelling the world), he said, "Zander, you have all the skills, you could accomplish anything that you really want to. Do you know the difference between where you're at and where I'm at?" And I said, "What?" He goes, "I've heard a million more noes than you have."'

Theo Davies, Head of Cloud Sales Enablement JAPAC, Google, remembers doing some maths on door-to-door sales:

> 'If I just knocked on a door, regardless of whether someone was there or not, I had just paid myself $4. If they opened the door, I picked up another $10. If I managed to get them to not slam the door, it went up to $50. So, I didn't care what happened.'

Breaking down your earnings in that way is possible in any job and really quite satisfying.

Embrace your failures

Katrin Kiviselg, Partner, NorthStar Consulting, says:

> 'I think that makes a difference with an experienced salesperson. We are not afraid of admitting our mistakes and looking back and really laughing at some of the bad stories. That's what makes people like me inspirational, more than anything. People love hearing me talking about my failures a lot more than they like hearing about my successes.'

My favourite sales debacle involved me dressing up like Princess Elsa from Disney's *Frozen* with two colleagues in Duracell bunny outfits dancing behind me and singing acapella to a rendition of 'Let it Sell (Duracell)' to the board of directors of a major UK retailer. (Our speaker malfunctioned.) Other brands had teams of puppies, chocolate fountains or alcoholic drink launches as part of their presentation, whereas what they got from us was a man in a dress, singing poorly. We didn't win the extra space we were bidding for, but people certainly like hearing the story!

KEY TAKEAWAY

'Noes' are not inherently bad, in fact, if you trust in the maths of sales (lesson 60), they are inherently good, so learn to embrace them.

11
Lessons On Managing Your Stakeholders

'The other challenge in a lot of sales environments is that they are often individually focused, and you still want a degree of that, but collaboration is the way we have won business. The average number of external decision-makers, according to the *Harvard Business Review*, is now 6.8 in business-to-business sales. Having one person selling to 6.8 people is reducing your chances massively.'
— Stuart Lotherington, MD, SBR Consulting

Lesson 76: Involving your team

The necessity of collaboration

In modern sales, no salesperson is an island. Especially in complex or intangible sales, it takes a team, led by an exceptional salesperson to sell effectively. Phil Burgess, Chief People Officer, C Space, says:

'For our salespeople, they have to have colla-boration skills. It's great if you have a salesperson that can just do it by themselves, but the reality is in our business they need to be able to pull in someone from the team who is going to help them have a sector perspective. They need to pull in someone else that is going to design the data solu-tion. They need to pull in something else from the creative team to help the proposal to look great. Some of our most successful salespeople are not necessarily the best salespeople with clients, but they are amazing internal collaborators. People want to help them. Some of our least success-ful salespeople, particularly in a complex cell where it might be half a million, a million dollars' worth of consulting, they are people who are not very good at collaborating internally.'

Nazia Khan, Business Development Manager, Outform, agrees:

'I live in a dream creative world where I create the opportunities, and then sometimes you get told internally, "We need more budget or... time." I've learned the operational team should be involved from the earliest stages of the selling, as soon as we've got a real opportunity, so they can cost up the projects and begin the operational journey in what needs to happen internally.'

How to best involve your team

Ronald Sluiter, Global Director, Gartner, has this advice:

> 'Salesmen work to discover needs; but if you go into too much detail when you are talking to people who have been CEOs for over twenty years, you can never match their knowledge on specific topics. I always want to make it clear that I'm a salesperson and that we have really distinguished roles between myself and the analysts. In the sales process, I'll ask an analyst to deep-dive on certain topics. They understand that, because they know I am a salesperson and I should not have all the answers. That is not my role.'

Dan Ingwell, Managing Partner, People Strategy Network, says:

> 'If I was doing another sales role, I'd really focus on the team aspect – when to bring in the expert, and when to bring in the boss. I see a lot of salespeople wheeling in the expert without getting anything back, and the customer saying, "Thanks very much for educating me and giving me all that expertise, but I have no intention of ever buying anything from you." I'd value my own resources better. I would take my subject matter experts out for a nice coffee and get them to like me. Then I'd call them up a week later and say, "Could you help me out and come to this customer with me,

please?" And they would, because we liked each other.'

KEY TAKEAWAY

Many of the best salespeople (lesson 21) are leaders. In complex sales, you have to be a leader as you are the main point of contact for a multifunctional team. To be exceptional, learn to co-ordinate the team's needs and build rapport internally.

Lesson 77: Selling well internally

Internal selling is unavoidable

While you should aim to do as little internal selling as possible (lesson 46), particularly in big corporates, it's unfortunately necessary to spend some time selling to internal stakeholders. As research by Salesforce has shown, salespeople unfortunately spend just one third of their time actually selling, with much of the remaining two thirds focused on internal tasks.[13] Minimising this time, and selling effectively, provides a huge competitive advantage.

13　T Bova, '26 sales statistics that prove sales is changing' (Salesforce, 2019), www.salesforce.com/blog/15-sales-statistics, accessed 16 November

Zander Fryer, CEO, High Impact Coaching, successfully sold his long-term vision to engineer a bigger sale:

> 'When you can be brave or courageous enough to have that real conversation, if you've got management above you, be like, "This is not the right thing to do here. If I'm clear with them, we'll be able to get them on a much bigger whale rather than this little fish." You could say, "Look, I'm not going to hit my quota this month, I'm not going to hit my quota this quarter, but I'm going to blow my number out of the water this year if you just let me do this." ... I remember I had to have that conversation with our director of operations. I had to tell him, "Look, we're not a good fit for this, which means we're going to lose out on this $3.5m deal." It's confidence, and it takes courage in your communication. Five months later, they ended up buying $22.5m worth of networking equipment from us.'

Nick Beresford, CEO, Enertor, has this advice:

> 'I would say be bold on the plans. Plans are usually... incremental and just small steps to growth and all businesses need rockets of growth. Set some big expectations internally and pitch to get the resources that you need to deliver. I also believe in keeping the numbers simple – never make long recommendations.'

Sharing your big goals with the business

Nick goes on to share an example:

'The other thing that we pitched at one point was called the "70% share Fairy plan". Fairy liquid had a 50% share of the UK washing-up liquid market for thirty years and just would not shift. Instead of saying, "Let's try for a 51% share," we said, "What would need to be true to get to a 70% share?" We came up with this 70% share plan where we put in extra investment in exchange for premium listings and display and sold it internally and externally. When I came off the brand, we'd grown ten share points in two years to 60%, and two years later, we actually hit the 70% share of the market, which for a big brand, which was already well-established, was unbelievable... That was compelling externally, but perhaps more importantly, internally.'

Selling yourself internally

Phil Burgess, Chief People Officer, C Space, says:

'I think that the people who collaborate and build relationships might be a little slower to begin with, but they ultimately sell more; make more money; hit their targets; and the teams are happier to bring them into conversations with clients because they see that their motives are not just, "I want to flog them the stuff," and more like, "I am going to work on their side and with you as well." I cannot think of many pitches where it is a solo effort. It usually involves five or six people, and the salesperson can choreograph all that.'

KEY TAKEAWAY

Since internal selling is inevitable, it makes sense to embrace it. Setting big goals can disproportionately get the business behind you, so get to know your stakeholders. Share news internally – in every business I've been in, I've shared either a weekly or monthly update on my personal or team results.

Lesson 78: Help develop your product

Salespeople are key to product development

Salespeople have unique insight into the product due to their constant interaction with prospects and clients. Henrietta Curtis, Head of Sales, React News, says:

'Passing on the feedback to our internal teams responsible for putting together the content for the events was important. We had specific feedback from multiple clients. A big part of the service was calling everybody after the event to get their feedback and their thoughts on subsequent programs and what they would like to see, what they thought went well and what didn't. It is a really important part of the sales process to keep people on board and engaged in what you're doing. It is critical because you are the filter between the client and the product itself. Feedback is integral to creating a product that fits what the clients are looking for and it also helps in keeping the role that you are doing fresh and interesting.'

Marketing and sales are closely interconnected, although many companies fail to recognise this. Phil Low, Growth Leader, Revolut, says:

'The word "marketing" is perceived to be, "Here's a product. Go and tell people about it." Much like sales is, "Go sell it." That's the fundamental misunderstanding of any good marketing or sales organisation. You need to have a constant feedback loop, incorporating qualitative and quantitative data for ongoing analysis; that feedback into your product organisation is invaluable.'

Failed sales as the best feedback

Lauri Kinkar, CEO, Messente Communications, tells a painful story of a decision by a client representing 40% of their business to leave them:

'They said, "We mean no offence, but we are leaving for a global operator. You seem to be a regional one at best." Boy did that hurt. I argued with them, and then went back home and it took me about a week to understand that they were 100% correct.

In terms of lessons, this was one of the biggest. I am now very thankful for the candid opinion. We ended up developing into more of a global operator just because of that sentence.'

Eric Hirschberg, CEO, Echo Finance, is always looking to learn from the 'noes':

> 'It makes sense to keep a Rolodex of people that have said "no" and return to them; to have a plan to re-engage them and approach them again, making sure to thank them. "Oh, great meeting. Thanks for… your time, I really learned a lot. I was thinking about what you were saying and if I got this right, you said this and does that mean this?"… You can often turn it around into a sale eventually.'

Selling unfinished products

The most extreme version of needing to give feedback to your product team is when the product is unfinished. Nazma Qurban, CRO, Cognism, relates such an experience:

> 'That is one of the first deals that I closed. We had a blackout which means that the product could not be shown. So, I go to the demo call, remain focused and describe the product vividly. I had to provide feedback to the organisation about what I had said and what the client had liked and we had to create the product closer to that vision.'

KEY TAKEAWAY

Regardless of your product life stage, you have every incentive to provide feedback on the product. Some internal stakeholders may not want to hear any negatives so you'll have to sell them (lesson 77) but you'll be doing the company and yourself a favour.

Lesson 79: Develop your customer relationships

The downside of not delivering

At one point, Peter Kiddle, Chairman, Business Transfer Agent, wondered where his sales were going. He says:

> 'I closed, they said yes, but it did not seem to materialise. What I learned from this is that getting the sale confirmed at the time is great, but you have got to see it through. I just left it too late because I was so busy, and by the time I managed to get time to give them a call another competitor had been there in the meantime and snatched it away from me. You have got to have a balance between good upfront sales activity and then securing it.'

Upside of great customer relationships

There are huge benefits to creating longstanding relationships. Russ Bloom, bond salesperson at a major bank, says:

> 'The call would come in, "Russ, I want to execute this bond, and everyone looks the same price. I'm giving this to you because I owe you a trade for past service." Don't be surprised how much people pay attention to what's deposited in the favour bank. It's an unspoken currency but on days when you think it's going slow, it comes through and pays you.'

Rich Kiddle, Director, Titanbay, had his current CEO give him this feedback:

> 'He recruited me because of my sales ability. He said that he gets called on a daily basis, but I was the only one who used the approach of, "Well, let's not do anything now. Let's just meet. Let's just work out whether this service is for you. If not, let's not bother and then maybe in the future something else will come up." I wanted to build the relationship in the long term. We met for a coffee and built rapport. He said no one had really made the effort to meet him before.'

Facetime, effort and non-pressure communication goes a long way.

How to win your customers over

Monica Hartman, Director, Gartner, has had a successful sales career by prioritising her client's needs:

> 'I also think that sometimes, the pressure of sales targets made me question some decisions as well, especially when you're in a sales environment where you're constantly wanting to hit a number and sell more. Sometimes I would find myself questioning and making sure that whatever I was doing was the right move for the client at the right time. I've always been able to do well, especially in the long term, by prioritising my clients' needs.'

How you talk and think about your clients is extremely important. Lauri Kinkar, CEO, Messente Communications, says:

> 'The way we think about people will show in our attitude and in our results as well. Sometimes you hear salespeople saying, "I have been trying to sell to those guys, but they really don't get it." In these cases, I always try to explain that if someone does not get your sales pitch, it's always your fault, not theirs. And if you do happen to screw up, admit you made a mistake.'

KEY TAKEAWAY

You might think that you'd have to choose between your clients and quota, but that wasn't the case for our exceptional interviewees, all of whom were top performers while providing exceptional service. Prioritising your customers will always pay dividends.

Lesson 80: Grow your network

How to get started

The idea of networking, especially when you're just starting out, can be daunting. Amanda Derham, Director, The Agile Director, gives an example:

> '[If you know] somebody who is looking for a new sales person and they do not know where to find them, and you know somebody who would be perfect for that job because of their personality traits, introduce them over a cup of coffee and make the suggestion… Making the right connections benefits them and it also benefits you. 'If you try this, you will see the flaws in your process and you can refine your process – you will have successes and you will have duds, and you will learn from both. You will learn more from the bad connections… by seeking feedback. Go to whoever you have introduced and say, "I was interested to see that you did not progress down that track. What stopped you?"'

Venetia Paske, Principal Consultant, SBR Consulting, says:

> 'Never feel that you are not senior enough to link in with that person that was in the meeting. If you were in that meeting, you can make it work with them. I think a lot of us have preconceived ideas about people maybe not wanting to respond or not wanting to introduce you, but if you have taken the time to nurture your network, people are really willing to offer introductions where they can help. Do not be afraid of using it.'

The best of networking

If you can get it right, having a great network can be lucrative. Zander Fryer, CEO, High Impact Coaching, says:

> 'When I quit Cisco, I had a company offer me a six-figure salary just to put my name on their records and make introductions. It would literally be a five- to ten-hour a week job. They were going to give me six figures just to make introductions because they knew the power of having a trust-worthy introduction.'

Saj Samiullah, Director, Quantribute, reveals how some great networking significantly helped his career:

> 'It turned out that I knew a couple of guys at this exclusive event that I had worked with already, so

naturally I joined them over lunch. The others saw me talking with them and… that's all I needed. Over the next month, I was approached by many of the people at that conference and have five clients off the back of that. Three of them represent my main revenue stream to this day, all from a moment as opposed to a year of cold calling and knocking on doors.'

Third-party validations

A great network has other significant benefits. Sam Lewis, Partner, Albourne Partners, explains who his most valuable ally is when recruiting new clients:

'It's the independent third party who has, for want of a better phrase, "drunk the Kool-Aid". Hopefully, they know what we're doing, and they like what we're doing, and critically, how we do it. That is more infectious in sales than anything else I've found.'

Will Ferrand, Global Director, Refinitiv, explains how his industry network helps him sell:

'Obviously, I'm not going to tell customer A that their biggest rival, customer B, is doing this but telling them, "I'm the one that's been out meeting clients the whole time," builds credibility. So, "Oh, I was speaking to someone the other day that was thinking about this…" and identifying industry trends and things so that you can add value to the conversation with them.'

KEY TAKEAWAY

Maintaining a quality network (lesson 83) vastly increases your success rate and makes you invaluable to the right business.

Lesson 81: Create business partnerships

An extra route to market

There were plentiful good examples of the interviewees using business partnerships to amplify their reach. Humphrey Bowles, Founder, Guardhog, says:

> 'Building partnerships – I think it's the most effective way of building a business from scratch. When it comes back to sales, building a partnership is also sales because it really comes down to finding a connection, getting in tune with your clients and then having the determination to keep on going and all that keeps the relationship moving forward. Get that first meeting. Get that first introduction by whatever means necessary.'

Rationale for partnerships

Alastair Ross, Founder, Codexx, uses partnerships for credibility:

'One of the first things I did was start studies with universities. I've got relationships with universities around looking at innovation in the legal sector, for example. Developing something unique and finding partners, because again, you've got to think like that if you're trying to be a thought leader. What's your legitimacy? Why would people believe what you say, rather than what somebody else says?'

Ilias Varth, CEO, Owiwi, says:

'Through recurring businesses and establishing relationships, you can also upsell and have other sorts of perks and benefits. Perhaps you want to do a customer success story with them. They will be much more willing to do it if they like you and they respect you for helping them accomplish their goals.'

Creativity in partnerships

Amanda Derham, Director, The Agile Director, has made a career out of creative partnerships:

'I do not paint; I do not sculpt. So that is my creativity. To connect people and see them work on something and go to the next level – that gives me satisfaction. One example was when I was involved in finding a sponsorship for an event focused on forty-plus-year-old women... There was a small salmon and aquaculture firm who were expanding and they wanted to target these women. There was a golf event at which they would all be, so I married the two together. That sponsorship was a wonderful meeting of a supplier who wanted to get to these people, and these people who would support a company who supported their sport. It worked really well.'

KEY TAKEAWAY

Having and creating partnerships that will sell for you and enhance your credibility can be enormously valuable. Some of the best commercial creativity I have seen involves partnering with a business with a similar client list to do more collective business, and you don't have to be a business owner to make it happen.

Lesson 82: Maintain your relationships

Maintaining relationships is key

Roger Philby, CEO, The Chemistry Group, says:

'I was taught a trick very early in my career and I teach it to everyone at Chemistry… If you meet anyone interesting and that is of a similar age where you think, "You are brilliant. I really like you," then write their name down in a notebook and make a commitment to call them every three months and say "Hi". Take the global head of talent at our major financial services client. I first met her when I was twenty-one. She was a junior HR business partner at a global soft drinks company and I was a nervous junior recruiter at Michael Page. It was my first proper client gig and we met and I really liked her… That one lady has spent upwards of two and a half million pounds with Chemistry over the last twenty years, and she has taken us with her to brewing and hospitality, banking and now information services. I still phone her every three months to chat and then she'll say, "Oh, by the way, I need to introduce you to someone." Thank you.'

The downside of non-maintenance

Dimitry Toukhcher, CEO, LGFG Fashion House, tells the sad story of losing a valued client:

'He said, "I am not buying it from you anymore." I said, "Why not?" He goes, "Because the last time you dropped off the suit for me, it was very wrinkly and it looked uncared for." It was a two-thousand-dollar suit. That was a lesson for me because I realised that I had failed at keeping his business. I did not treat him to the standard he deserves to be treated as a client, with that kind of money he was spending, and the kind of trust he was giving me.'

Rich Kiddle, Director, Titanbay, shares a lesson he learned about maintaining relationships:

> 'I got back in touch with him six months later, which was the timeframe he had agreed on and I think I was quite shirty about it when I said I wasn't budging on any pricing. I was quite abrupt with them. I re-explained how a previous sales process was a bit unfair on us; they were taking stuff from us and not coming back to the table. I essentially lost the sale because they didn't like the way I went about business – something I won't do again.'

As a salesperson, a short memory and graciousness will serve you well.

The litmus test of true relationships

Roger Philby, CEO, The Chemistry Group, says:

> 'The thing is that as a salesperson you need to see yourself as an independent business. Your value is who you know, because what you know will change. I find this amazing that we hire client partners who have been in the corporate world for twenty-five or thirty years and they are like, "Yeah, I've got a great network." Then they come in and I am like, "Right. So, if you have a great network, this is your fourth week, you should have brought a client in by now." They do not have great networks. They have lots of people on LinkedIn that they kind of know but because they have not

been purposeful about building their network and the value of their network, it does not work.'

KEY TAKEAWAY

Meeting people is important but prioritising, organising and having the discipline to maintain these relationships once made is key to exceptional sales.

12
Lessons On Avoiding Career Pitfalls

'What would I do differently? Probably everything. I think I would take more time to do more research. I think I would apply myself a little differently. One of the sales books I have got here that I have been reviewing, they talk about Warren Buffett. He reads five hundred pages a day; and perhaps we all should. An education will give you a job. Learning on the job will give you a career.'

— Jeremy Jacobs, The Sales Rainmaker®

Lesson 83: Get your motivation and environment right

Skill and will

Lars Tewes, Director, Clean Living International, recalls key learnings on motivation from his sales training days:

'For many years we talked about the terms "skill" and "will"... A lot of salespeople are highly skilled, but do not want to work hard anymore. Equally, a lot of people are highly motivated, but lack the skill to ask great questions, listen to the prospect and recommend the right solution. Both skill and will are necessary; having one or the other is not enough to succeed. From a skill side, you need to map which activities are going to give you the most success and then continually focus on those. For example, if you play tennis and you are losing matches because you are double-faulting a lot, then that is something you need to work on. Sales is the same – if you are getting lots of meetings but they are not converting into proposals, you need to change something in your meeting or your follow-up. From the will side, it really is about making sure you set the right goals and targets for yourself. If you are not feeling personally motivated, then revisit your goals.'

Choose your support network

Andrew Santos, CEO, Compass Group, reflects on why some salespeople fail:

'Negative financial pressure, and lack of support from people they know. Their sphere of influence, their spouse. If someone comes into my business as a salesperson and they come home at night and their spouse is like, "How much did you sell?" and they have to say, "I did not get on the board today," and the spouse is like, "I knew this was a bad idea," that is not going to work out very well. Your spouse needs to be on board. Their support structure needs to be on board.'

Kristen Gonzalez, VIP Brand Promoter, Thrive, says:

'I would also try to block out all the noise around me and put some blinders. It affects me when people would say things like, "Oh… you're going into network marketing, those things never work out," or, "Are you selling vitamins? I'm sure it's just a placebo." Or someone in the family tells me, "You're had a good career in education and you're going to do something that you don't know if it's going to work out or not?" Try to block out the noise early on and not listen to the naysayers. Block out some of the negativity that we all have around us.'

Surround yourself with top people

Ron Alford, Senior Partner, Southwestern Consulting, reveals how he finds the best people to surround himself with:

'Look under rocks if you have to, look in trees, bushes, whatever you got to do, man, and find them, because it's worth it… And no, it doesn't mean I judge those that aren't in that category. It's just I've got this highly selective eye for this core group.'

I was incredibly lucky to be surrounded by top people during my first summer selling door-to-door. We helped each other with attitude (lesson 59), ensured our statistics were strong (lesson 60), and made what should have been an awful time a great one. The result of that mutual support was that our household sold more in total than any other household of salespeople that summer, for which I am eternally grateful.

KEY TAKEAWAY

There's no escaping the fact that the people around you affect your thinking and your mood. Ensure those people are supportive of your selling success.

Lesson 84: Don't take it personally

'No' is not a disaster

Andrew Santos, CEO, Compass Group, says:

'I would say when you hear "no" constantly, that means you are doing it right... When I was young in the business, I'd hear all these "noes" and just get obsessed with them and just want to hear "yes". Then you realise, "Wait a minute, I did pretty well." So those "noes" are just part of the process – you have to embrace them. If you hear "no" a ton, you are doing it right. When you really disconnect your soul and your personal desires of earning money, you create the space to be pleasantly persistent and not offend people. They can tell that you are cool with a "no". When you are really and truly to the core OK with hearing "no", you will start to do well.'

Howard Paine, Regional Sales Manager, Zscaler, says:

'I stepped back and realised, "Actually, no one's going to die." Nothing terrible is really going to happen – the worst-case scenario is you lose your job and find another one. I think keeping that emotional distance from the outcome of sales is fantastic, however you do that, be it through other hardships, other important causes to you, or other things. The more you act as if you don't care, as if you're not emotionally connected, the better your calls will be.'

Zander Fryer, CEO, High Impact Coaching, says:

'Don't just be OK with failure and rejection and hearing the word "no". Actually look for it. Desire it… Desire faster and bigger failure and you will grow bigger and faster as well.'

Eric Hirschberg, CEO, Echo Finance, explains the importance of embracing 'noes'. He says:

'It's important to have the ability to embrace "no" and understand that objection is a good thing… If

it's "yes" and they've got a pen and they're sign-
ing, great, but "no" is a very close second best in
terms of results. It allows you to say, "You know,
listen, I know you don't want this, and I respect
that, but can you do me the favour of explaining
why you don't want it, and maybe I can learn
something from that process?" After time, that will
turn into a sale.'

Provide value to everyone

Radoslav Ivanov, International Sales Executive, Historical Park Bulgaria, has a great attitude towards sales:

'It is going to be worth people's while even if they
buy or not. They are going to feel enriched after
they speak to me. Selling is the transfer of feelings
and emotions. I want people to feel great after they
speak with me. I do not care if they buy or not.
That is not up to me; I cannot control that.'

True buying atmosphere

A good 'buying atmosphere' is when a prospect feels
completely comfortable saying 'no', which paradoxi-
cally, increases the chance of them saying 'yes'.

Vlada Tusco, Partnerships Manager at a large international media company, says:

'Having a "mindset of abundance" also helps. I
am OK with people saying "no" because there are

opportunities everywhere out there… I genuinely do not mind not getting the sale. If I am going to get the sale or the deal, it has to be right, and it has to be the right story, it has to be the right opportunity for them, and it needs to be right for everybody.'

KEY TAKEAWAY

Since you will inevitably deal with thousands of 'noes' in your sales career – tens of thousands if you desire to be exceptional – don't take it personally and make sure everyone walks away having seen the best of you.

Lesson 85: Be about others, not yourself

The best presentations

'It's hard to be nervous when your mind is on service' is an expression I've been continuously reminded of while summoning the will to pick up the phone and dial. If you can provide value outside of just the 'yes/no' decision, your sales interactions will be more effective and more fun for both yourself and your prospects.

Richard Humphreys, ex-CEO, Saatchi & Saatchi, says:

'You're trying to get your character across, your ability to understand them. In my experience, the best way to start that process is not really to talk about yourself, or your company, but to talk about their company. The most successful presentations I've ever made, I don't think I mentioned our advertising agency at all. I just talked about whatever they really wanted to know. I think if you're interested in them, they become interested in you.'

Greg James, financial advisor at a major US bank, discusses the importance of prioritising clients' interests above:

'I spend much of my time talking people out of decisions. That's something you don't hear in the media – how really good financial advisors will tell people not to do things if it's not the right thing for the client. There is a lot of that because you feel some responsibility to help them make decisions to move them toward their financial goals.'

Stay humble and get second chances

It's essential not to get caught up in your own achievements and to stay humble. Rupert Warburton, CEO, Caffe Kix, says:

'Sometimes when things are going well, it's easy to take the credit without understanding the underlying causes, which might be outside your control.

There are a lot of large, powerful players in my sector. I remember not winning a particular cafe because I think I was a bit cocky, a bit arrogant, in the way I conducted the process. I think I just sort of assumed that it was coming to me and it didn't. So never assume.'

Ryan Dowd, Business Development Manager, COMATCH, reflects on a deal that was disappointing at first:

'We did not end up winning that deal. They ultimately went with somebody who was already in their pipeline, but subsequently imploded and regretted that, because they should have let it breathe a bit more. A month later, the same client was so pleased with the way we served her the first time, even knowing we were coming from behind with the acknowledgement of that, that she wanted to give us the first chance.'

KEY TAKEAWAY

It's easy to get emotionally involved in a sales process but that's likely to be detrimental to your results. Remaining service-minded and humble will ultimately win the day.

Lesson 86: Sell to the decision-makers

The fiasco of getting power wrong

Josef Dvorak, Country Manager, SBR Consulting, tells the all-too-familiar story of his deal getting quashed by the true decision-makers:

> 'I was talking to three division directors. There was a CEO as well, so four decision-makers in total. I sold the idea to the three division directors well and thought that was enough. Well, actually, I didn't think it was enough, but my inner dialogue persuaded me that to sell the idea to the CEO was too much outside my comfort zone – the three division directors would sell it to him. I came up with an excuse that three out of four was enough and invested about two and a half months in this deal. Then the CEO came and crushed the whole thing because he wasn't personally sold on the idea. That taught me that it's better to be outside my comfort zone at the beginning of the process rather than feeling the pain of regret at the end. I "should have, could have, would have" talked to him and got over that feeling of discomfort. It was a huge lesson. I've never done it since.'

Mike Turner, MD, YouBecome, understands this pain:

> 'Multiple times we thought that the sale was in the bag, but because we were being sponsored

and promoted by the HR team we would get to the close just to be told that the directors or the CEO don't want to do it, they wanted to invest in something else. It's all about the decision-making authority. Identifying exactly who all the players were. I made those mistakes – there were multiple painful experiences.'

On tenders

Tenders, or 'request for proposal' (RFP), are the worst form of not reaching the decision-maker and to be avoided if possible. Jonathan Hamer, ex-law firm partner, saw a lot of tenders:

> 'Sometimes, halfway through, you had an awful feeling that you were only there because they thought they should go and get two or three firms to pitch for the job rather than because they had any interest in using a firm other than the one they always use.'

Scott Roy, CEO, Whitten & Roy, says:

> 'RFPs are a rubbish process, quite frankly. We teach salespeople not to engage with them unless one of two things are true: one, your company did the research that the RFP is based upon. You have a high chance of winning that bid and a high degree of certainty you will deliver it to spec and brilliantly. Or two, someone else did the research, but you ask for and are granted access to the people that

have the problem upon which the RFP is based. In this case you are able to learn about the problems first-hand, engage with the client personally, and challenge the thinking in the RFP if warranted. It gives you an inside track to understand if you can actually deliver what they want and if it's worth your time and effort to submit a proposal.'

If there's no way to avoid RFPs then you must play the game, but in my experience, they are a recipe for delay, discord and disappointment for both sides.

Aim to meet the decision-maker

Aim to somehow reach the decision-makers and pitch to them directly. Alastair Ross, Founder, Codexx, says:

'I want to have a meeting with the key people, whether it's a senior partner or a director or the head of the business unit you're discussing. If you can't get access to those sorts of people then it says a lot about their ability or willingness to do something. Sometimes you only get discussions at a local level. These people might help lead you somewhere else, but sometimes they can't get you any further access. They're just trying to learn at your expense.'

Connie Smith, Consultant, Whitten & Roy, says:

'I realised that it is so crucial to find out right at the beginning of every sale who makes the decisions and not be scared to ask, not make assumptions. The other thing is to not be scared to speak to the person who is causing the problems in a business. It is really important to understand their side of the story.'

Carolin Berger, Regional Sales Manager, Outpost24, cautions, 'There is always someone else. There is always someone that is also influencing the decision, and if you have not met them, then the competitor probably has.'

KEY TAKEAWAY

Not selling to the decision-maker was the most common reason that our interviewees gave in their cautionary tales of failed sales, with twenty-four such stories told. Learn from their mistakes and find out who can wield the pen to give you that sale.

Lesson 87: Avoid complacency

The risk of being comfortable

The biggest battle for some our interviewees was avoiding complacency, losing their 'will' (lesson 83) as their skill levels peaked. Manny Gonzalez, Financial Advisor, Raymond James, says this about his past:

'Once I got going, man, I got going, but then I got comfortable, and I relied on my talents versus the hard work that got me there – it's happened to me twice. When I started this career, I said, "All right, I know what's going to happen, I've been through it before, I cannot let myself get to that position again." It's complacency – you've never made it, the moment you think you've made it, that's the danger zone because now you've stopped growing, you stop developing, you stop having fresh ideas, and you're starting to go backwards, so for a salesperson, complacency is your biggest killer.'

Stuart Lotherington, MD, SBR Consulting, says:

'In my first sales career, I stayed for ten years but I wish I had moved sooner. For me, it is about learning. One of my core values is learning and for you to be successful, you need to be learning. I would say that if you are not learning and you have achieved a good degree of performance, then you should move.'

Focus on becoming invaluable

Perhaps the biggest motivation to keep growing is the desire to become invaluable and essential to an organisation, which will guarantee you future employment. Kristel Tuul, Growth Marketer, Consultant, shares how she became increasingly invaluable:

'I think the key is how fast you can learn. Do not look at your sales and how you are doing as a success or a failure, or that you are weak or strong; look at it as an option to learn or not learn. When I started my sales career, I was average. I remember in my first two weeks I sold nothing. I am one of the few that grew every single year, and soon I was in the top 5% three years in a row. I was not talented and immediately got it – it was all learning. I think that is why I did well in tech and marketing. That is the main piece of advice: to learn, to have a growth mindset and to keep learning skills.'

Russ Bloom, bond salesperson at a major bank, says:

'You need to think of your sales techniques because this is your franchise, and whoever you're working for, that's just the current logo on your pay cheque. Your opinion and your reputation will travel with you. My father was in sales, and that was one thing he always told me when I was a little kid – there's only one thing that you take a lifetime to build and five seconds to destroy, and that's your reputation. If there's one thing you're going to protect, it's that; every day and all day.'

KEY TAKEAWAY

In the act of progressing, there is no time to stand still. If you need to build your franchise, ensure you never get complacent.

Lesson 88: Know your worth

Negotiate big

One of the biggest regrets of many interviewees is that they didn't negotiate hard enough upfront in a new job – it's much harder to negotiate once you're in it. Richard Kiddle, Director, Titanbay, says:

> 'Take your time when reviewing an opportunity. I often felt rushed; I felt pressured by the recruiter and by the company. If you are a good candidate, if you have the confidence, then be the one they want just as much as you want them. If you have ownership in a business or you do financial exams or you build trusting, long-term relationships over time, you will be wealthier than you would be if you try and get a higher base salary from the start.'

Theo Davies, Head of Sales Enablement JAPAC, Google, says:

> 'I've seen people work really hard, build up knowledge and skills within a company, and then become frustrated at not getting paid what they're worth because they didn't have that extra incentive agreed beforehand and the company has discretion as to how much of the commission they give them. I think that kind of stuff can be pre-agreed as an understanding with a direct manager – "Hey, what if I hit my quota and then I exceed it by 100%,

can we talk about how much extra I would make?" In other words, "If I double my number, can we negotiate on a banded approach to commission?"'

Build your self-belief

Jason Walkingshaw, Partner, S.G.F.E, says:

'I wish I had believed in myself more because I think one of the biggest things that separate top salespeople from the rest is their belief levels. They have such confidence in what they can do and it probably took me a couple of years in order for me to kind of get to that level. Top performers at almost any level now, if you think about sportspeople, they build a habit and get used to those habits of always accomplishing things and breaking down belief barriers.'

Josef Dvorak, Country Manager, SBR Consulting, gradually broke his own belief barriers:

'What I found quite challenging (and proved myself to be wrong) is that it's going to be quite difficult to sell to a partner from the Big Four who is in his fifties when I'm in my thirties and advising them how to sell. We were able to do it here very successfully and continue doing so, so I guess age probably doesn't matter as much as I thought at the beginning.'

Value your time

Dimitry Toukhcher, CEO, LGFG Fashion House, says:

> 'If you give any indication to the prospect that your time is free, they are going to cheat you of it. "Oh, come back tomorrow. Oh, give me a call later. Send me an email…" You need to learn how to negotiate your time. You need to learn how to negotiate your value.'

Corbin McGuire, MD, RNM Recruiting, reflects on the most successful individuals he knows:

> 'I would say really successful people have this different view. The really good ones are a little bit more prideful; they have a little bit more respect for themselves. What I mean by that is that they will look to be innovative rather than do the same thing over and over and over, because doing the same thing over and over is hard and you can do better if you innovate.'

Zander Fryer, CEO, High Impact Coaching, helps various types of coaches correctly position their value:

> 'They often position themselves as a commodity. When they try and charge a hundred bucks an hour but Weight Watchers are charging thirty dollars a month, they're forever out of luck. When you realise that this coach can actually help you get unbelievable results – we have several of our clients that can literally help you heal autoimmune

disorders like Hashimoto's, PCOS, Crohn's dis-
ease – [disorders] that doctors are telling people
are unhealable... and people are telling them... a
hundred bucks or two hundred bucks a month is
too expensive?'

KEY TAKEAWAY

If you downgrade the value of your time and required
compensation, others will too. The way you frame
your value in terms of being willing to take variable
compensation (lesson 47), providing exceptional results
and improving the culture (lesson 93) can ensure you're
rewarded appropriately.

Lesson 89: Know when it's time to move on

The argument to stick it out

While the temptation is to move early and often
in your career, many of our interviewees advised
patience. Ron Alford, Senior Partner, Southwestern
Consulting, says:

'Many people I've gotten to work with over the
years just wanted it quick, and if they didn't get it,
whether its sales as a career or a certain company
or a certain product, they just jumped to another.
They think the grass is always greener [elsewhere],
but the grass is greenest where you water it. Water

the damn grass where you're standing and where you're at now. I'm not saying there's not a time and a place to leave and do something different, but I think patience is important.'

Reasons to move on: effectiveness and happiness

There are sometimes good reasons to move. John Schlegel, CEO, Stonebridge Search, relates why he left a previous job:

'The guy says to me, "John, I have to tell you something, and I really mean this with great respect. If you keep doing this, I'll probably keep buying stuff from you just because I like you, but I think you deserve to know this – you're not good at this." The way he said it was heartfelt and sincere, and he went on, "I really have tried to give you the benefit of the doubt here. I'm trying to work with you. I just have to tell you I'm not sure this is for you." It was time to leave.'

Rich Kiddle, Director, Titanbay, shares his experience in a previous role:

'People were saying, "Well, you sound quite unhappy." I had a really frank conversation with myself: "What has changed? Has my drive changed? Why am I not happy? I've got this job that I always wanted. I have always wanted to be in finance, in a high-paying job, with the potential to be paid multimillions." But I was not happy. I think it is just knowing when to pull the trigger and having conversations with people that you trust, and just laying it all out. I wrote everything on a page: the strengths, weaknesses, opportunities, threats – not in those exact brackets but a similar model. The result was more in favour for me to leave than to stay. The opportunities where I am now completely outweighed the risks of leaving.'

If you determine that you should leave in such an objective way, you may well be correct.

Reason to move on: learning

You need to ensure you can keep learning in your current role. Stuart Lotherington, MD, SBR Consulting, has his regrets:

'In my first sales career, I stayed for ten years and I wish I had moved sooner. For me, it is about learning. One of my core values is learning and for you to be successful, you need to be learning. I would say that if you are not learning and you have achieved a good degree of performance, then you should move.'

Felipe Poveda, Head of Sales EMEA, CreditSights, agrees:

'You can do it for a short period for the role itself, for the content and the money. But once you're done learning, you'll probably have the inclination to move on. If you don't, then eventually you will feel like you've wasted time before you moved.'

Reason to move on: when it's statistically time

There is science behind when you should move on in a typical sales role as well. Slim Earle of The Chemistry Group explains:

'Sales is a challenging world to enter and survive, but typically when you look at tenure and performance, you tend to see a two-year slow incremental increase, then the second to seventh year is the peak performance, and then post-seven years, you see quite a significant downturn. Clearly, a lot of attrition happens in years one and two, so organisations might be losing lots of great potential in there because people do not persevere and there is a breakthrough moment in those first twenty-four months which then enables peak performance for those next four, five, six years or so. When you look at that from a career perspective, our clients often worry about good and bad churn. That might help them predict that even though this person is high-performing, they are close to that seven-year window and whether that might start to drop off and actually a change would be good for them.'

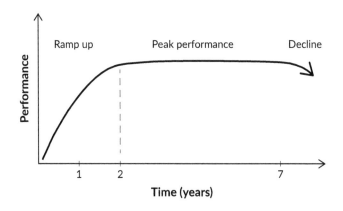

Sales effectiveness

KEY TAKEAWAY

If you're genuinely unhappy, if you're not growing or it's been seven-plus years, then sales gives you the freedom and flexibility to move on should you choose to (lesson 15). Choose the path of most advancement and continue to become exceptional.

13
Lessons On Becoming Exceptional

'There is no key to success in sales... If you are to truly be invaluable to an organisation, you need to be a rainmaker who is also a team player. It's the combination lock.'
— Theo Davies, Head of Cloud Sales Enablement JAPAC, Google

Lesson 90: Set huge goals, then break them down

How to set huge, achievable goals

You need to first set big goals before you can aim to hit them. Wade Shealy, CEO, Thirdhome, details the challenging steps to achieving goals:

'The first step is studying their goals or having aspirations. I'd say most people do that, not everybody, but most people have some kind of goal or some kind of aspiration. Most people don't write them down but they've got them in their head. That's stage one. The second thing is a detailed plan of how they are going to reach those goals and aspirations. Very few people like getting the details and planning how they're going to make those goals and aspirations come to fruition. The last thing is forming the habit of doing the things that they have to do to reach their goals and aspirations and to follow that plan. Almost nobody forms those habits, and the ones who do are very successful.'

Lars Tewes, Director, Clean Living International, says:

'Most companies talk about setting SMART [Specific, Measurable, Achievable, Realistic, Timely] goals… However, I have always felt that they were designed for the boardroom and for big corporations because they do not tell the whole story of an individual. Human beings are motivated by logic *and* emotion. SMART goals are based around logic only. Our approach to goal setting has been to help salespeople have logical goals but to also understand the emotions behind them. On top of the SMART elements, they also need to ask themselves two questions to see if it really motivates them: "If I do achieve the goal, what will I gain? If I do not achieve the goal, what will happen?"'

Theo Davies, Head of Cloud Enablement JAPAC, Google, says:

'Something I learned was the power of preparation. They would always talk about the "6Ps" in South-western: proper planning and preparation pre-vents pitiful performance. I remember writing a 100,000-word thesis on how I was going to break the company record. I would run up Arthur's Seat, a tall hill in Edinburgh, repeating and visualising my goals. All of that was prior to the year that I did it – it took an enormous amount of preparation and I think most people don't do that.'

If you put effort into your goal setting, you'll reap some serious rewards, as the success of these sales-people attests.

Exceed your goal setting

To hit these high goals, you're going to have to break your own belief barriers and go above and beyond. Nick Beresford, CEO, Enertor, explains his rationale behind huge goals:

'You look at these ultra-marathon runners and at one stage, somebody had never run more than 40 miles in a race. Now there have been a million peo-ple. It's cases like Roger Bannister's four-minute mile – it took sixty years to break it and then in six months three more people did it. It's just about expectations and believing that you can break it. Once you're clear about it, it is possible – nine times out of ten or ninety-nine times out of a hundred, those things are possible.'

Robin Mukherjee, MD, 2Circles Consulting, believes in ensuring you go further:

'The first thing is to set high goals and decide what you want to do. Then ensure that those high goals include doing more than was asked of you. I've always done more than was asked of me. If I was asked to do forty interviews, I'd do fifty. I always set higher goals because I always figured that would give me an edge over all my competition. So, set really high goals and then exceed them.'

Break them down

Large goals can be daunting, so breaking them down into manageable chunks is good practice. Nazma Qurban, CRO, Cognism, says:

'What can you achieve daily? What can you achieve weekly? Do not stretch to monthly because it is very easy to get lax and defer activity. What made me successful was that I had these mini-goals and benchmarks that I had to achieve daily because you just break everything down to that level. It is a lot easier to achieve those mini-goals than the entire picture. If you are focused on the future, you are going to actually neglect the present, and it's your activity in the present that is going to get you there.'

Rusty Branch, President, Compass Law, was told by a US governor:

> 'It's exactly the same principle that we learned selling books door-to-door. It's exactly the same principle running for governor, and it's exactly the same principle recruiting law firm partners. You just go to work every day. You take it one step at a time. You keep following the system, following the success principles that we know. It's hard by the yard; it's a cinch by the inch.'

KEY TAKEAWAY

You're almost guaranteed not to break records if you don't set them as committed goals and then break them down into manageable, controllable levels of activity that you can do every day. Set exceptional daily goals that add up to something amazing.

Lesson 91: Find a way to never give up on your goals

It won't be easy

To hit your goals, you need to be fully committed. Dimitry Toukhcher, CEO, LGFG Fashion House, says:

> 'I certainly had my fears, my doubts and other things when I was younger. However, I was not going to walk away as a loser, I was going to walk

away as a winner. I am not talking about being "the number one rookie in the Eastern Division of the lower half of the city among males who are under six foot five, but more than six foot..." I am not talking about narrowly defining something to inflate the actual results. If you are going to walk away, walk away as a winner – a true winner.'

Theo Davies, Head of Cloud Enablement JAPAC, Google, tells a story about one of his worst days in door-to-door sales and how he committed to being his best:

'I was sitting outside the church and I hadn't sold anything all day, and I hadn't sold anything the day before. I was calculating how much I'd been paid per hour – pretty easy, it was zero. I was on straight commission and I remember I didn't even know where to go. I had made a commitment not to ever go home during the work day... and I remember thinking, "I can go to a church. Church is always open right there, always willing to welcome you." I remember going to the church and even that the church was locked. I made a decision at that moment – I remember it like it was yesterday. I didn't care if I didn't get paid. I had committed to doing this and I was going to do it no matter what... We had 800 rookies in the company. I was going to be number one rookie, and I wasn't exactly anywhere close at that point. I thought, "You know what, it doesn't matter if I didn't make anything today or if I don't for the rest of the week. I've committed to do this, no matter what."'

You need momentum

Corbin McGuire, MD, RNM Recruiting, says:

> 'You just have to stay positive, encouraged and driven to do your task. Everything starts with attitude. If you are in a CrossFit gym… which has created that culture and attitude, you are going to hit your reps regardless of the degree of difficulty. You have people cheering for you, encouraging you, you don't want to fail those people – your environment helps you create reps when you didn't think you had any more reps to give. Each rep gives you more data. The hardest part about sales is keeping someone energised while they are capturing data through discovering what doesn't work.'

Kristen Gonzalez, VIP Brand Promoter, Thrive, notes:

> 'It's really too bad when people get… rejected or they come across problems they don't know how to solve and they just throw in the towel and give up on themselves way too quickly when they're probably right on the brink of success and if they had just stuck it out a little bit longer, they'd be excelling.'

Find a way

Sometimes you just need to find a way to get into winning situations. Saj Samiullah, Director, Quantribute, says:

'I've learned that if I can get in front of people, face-to-face, we win more business in recruitment. The conversion rate when I'm face-to-face is massive, close to 100%, but getting your voice heard is difficult. It's about finding ways to have a face-to-face conversation in a marketplace that doesn't really want you to do that. I've engineered ways of getting into conferences where recruiters shouldn't be… Then from a five-minute snippet over a break or sitting down with someone at lunch, I get a chance to do what I do best, which is talking to people.'

Ronald Sluiter, Global Director, Gartner, tells the story of a last-minute sale, which he needed to hit his annual goal, but the signatory was already on holiday:

'I found out which hotel he was staying at and I called the reception at eight o'clock in the morning… He was about to ski with his family, and then… reception said, "We have a phone call for you." He picked up, and he started laughing. He said, "OK, I made some promises. I did not do it. I understand. You've got five minutes to send it via fax." In five minutes, the fax was signed, as was my return to the President's Club incentive. Those things you will remember – if you have a commitment from both sides, you can call people at the end of the quarter or the year.'

KEY TAKEAWAY

Incredible perseverance, having prior agreements (see lesson 67), and great self-talk (lesson 97) can ensure you always find a way to hit your goals.

Lesson 92: Be a cultural asset

Risks of a salesperson on culture

As a top salesperson, you will have a disproportionate effect on company culture and morale. Corbin McGuire, MD, RNM Recruitment, acknowledges:

'I had one guy tell me one time, "Hey, your energy is so contagious that when you're positive you bring magic to our culture so that it drives our team, but when you're negative you bring such toxicity that you literally harm our sales." He continued, "I don't mean to be rude by telling you this. I'm just going to ask you – we've decided as a company we'll continue to pay you if you'll stay at home on those days that you think you'll be negative."'

Be a good person

Being a great salesperson isn't the same as being a great person. Dimitry Toukhcher, CEO, LGFG Fashion House, found out the hard way:

'You have to clearly define your standards. I failed all that before because I was like, "Oh, they sell well," but they were terrible human beings. That's a recipe for disaster. Yeah, you are going to definitely win in the short run, but boy, are you going to pay for it in the long run. What happens is the people that are not terrible human beings all see it and they leave, and then eventually you just have a bunch of terrible people and you do not want that.'

Ollie Venn, Operations Director, Foxtons, has a solution. 'We have a saying in the office, "Be the person on the other end of the phone that whomever you're calling remembers that day." Sales is a transfer of enthusiasm.'

Teach others

Radoslav Ivanov, International Sales Executive, Historical Park Bulgaria, says:

'I know I am lying if I am not doing what I am teaching people to do. I am constantly asking people, "Hey, what is your self-talk? What do you like to say to yourself when you feel down?"… There are young people that haven't yet learned what I have. I keep myself accountable to the people that I train and teach and that is why I cannot stop self-talking all the time.'

KEY TAKEAWAY

Nearly all of our interviewees were teachers or mentors in some way, which helps to cement them as invaluable to their organisation. With some consideration and attitude control (lesson 59), you can ensure you're as good to your organisation as you are to yourself.

Lesson 93: Be creative and memorise stories to tell

Why stories?

Many interviewees wove stories and anecdotes throughout their interview answers, often without even realising it. This is not to say it wasn't a learned trait, however.

Roger Philby, CEO, The Chemistry Group, says:

'I've learned to tell a story that is so good that they want to tell their wife or their husband that story when they walk through the door that evening. Be memorable. What I want to leave them with is, "Did you know this?" I don't want them to tell their colleagues, "I met a talent firm that we are going to be using." I want them to leave the meeting and say, "I met this freaking cool company today. They are going to be doing our talent."'

Lee McCroskey, speaker, trainer and coach, Southwestern Speakers, says:

> 'If you can tell a story like, "Let me tell you about what my wife is dealing with," then people understand you, especially if the person you are trying to reach out to is a relationship-oriented person… If I am calling on somebody who is a detailed person who does not really care about stories, then testimonials of what other people said about the product would be better. If they just want the data, then I'm going to give them the data.'

How to tell a story

Storytelling is an art with a hint of science. Stuart Lotherington, MD, SBR Consulting, shares his secrets:

> 'I think a good story is connecting it to yourself, which is why they are all personal stories. It is also about understanding how a person is receiving your story. What is going on from their signals? Then, building the picture of that situation so that people can actually visualise themselves doing that kind of thing. "Facts tell, stories sell." I think it is just a learned thing. You learn to use third-person validation the whole time, you weave in stories and this makes it visual for people and makes it resonate.'

Ron Alford, Senior Partner, Southwestern Consulting, gives an example of a story he might use that resonates with a prospect:

> 'Yesterday I had a call from a client and he was just saying, man, his team is seasoned, they're so dang sharp, they know what to do, but they're just like going through the motions – some of them are like waiting for business to come to them versus getting out and hunting. I don't know, for you Jamie, do you guys feel that? Is that at all something you can relate to with your team? Building tension, character development and conflict are all key elements of telling a powerful story.'

Using ingenuity to sell

Sometimes you need to innovate to get a prospect's attention. Here are a few examples for inspiration. Stuart Lotherington, MD, SBR Consulting, says:

> '[A colleague] had a great example once. Coming out of a client meeting where they had talked about their growth and learning that they were moving into a new building, he literally took a picture of himself outside the new building and sent it to the client as a follow-up saying, "We want to help you move into this building fast." This kind of creativity just melts barriers.'

Richard Humphreys, ex-CEO, Saatchi & Saatchi, says:

'My most successful pitch was when we presented for an account, a substantial potential account which was a seller of cars. We left behind just a postcard. The postcard had the creative image that we wanted to get across, with the strapline "nothing on earth comes close" because the company also made aeroplanes. All that was on the card was the name of the agency and "nothing on earth comes close" – and we won the business.'

Theresa Sproul, Sales Leader, Tom James, tells her favourite story of how she turned a sale around and sold a full suit when a prospect had selected only a single shirt:

'I said to him, "OK, can I make a recommendation? Let's say, if you were to go to a really nice steakhouse. Your friends told you about it, you've never tried it, and you go and you ask for a sweet tea. That's it. I don't want to try anything else. I just want a sweet tea. They bring it to you and you try it. It's all right, but that's never going to get you to go back to that restaurant again. It makes a lot more sense to order a steak. Same here. Don't just order a shirt from me. You're going to wait for a long time for a shirt or you can buy the whole outfit, a full suit." He smiled and said, "OK, go on then."'

KEY TAKEAWAY

What do these stories have in common? They are examples of driving impact home through visual, innovative stories and media. Start collecting memorable stories and learn to tell them brilliantly.

Lesson 94: Really own your industry

Find your niche

It's fine to move around early and even often in your early career (see lesson 25), but eventually you need to settle into your niche. Charles Talbot, MD, Pinpoint Partners, says:

> 'It probably takes three to five years to develop a network to the position where you can become the number one or a top name in the market that you focus on. The time that this takes comes down to the ever-present juggle between specialism and depth and focus. You can become a specialist in the smaller market much quicker. But then, of course, you risk focusing on too narrow a market and not having enough opportunities for sales.'

Dan Ingwell, Managing Partner, People Strategy Network, notes that the industry barriers for sales-people are now higher than ever:

'Salespeople are expected to have done their homework… and already understand the main industry issues. What are the main issues and measures that a person of this job role is likely to be struggling with? The skill for a salesperson has increased in that respect.'

Saj Samiullah, Director, Quantribute says:

'I can talk to the candidates, that's my strongest point. I am, at heart, still a candidate working in IT. My skills set me apart by winning their trust. A recruiter coming in who doesn't have a technology background can't talk technically, whereas someone going into accountancy recruitment will take about six weeks to learn the buzzwords and have some credibility speaking to someone. They can do it even if they don't have the background, but it will take longer to win their trust, and it'll be more of a numbers game. With me, it's not just a numbers game.'

Become a foremost expert

Developing your expertise is a prerequisite to be exceptional, as these interviewees attest. Thomas Haas of a large SaaS company says:

'From my perspective, as a buyer, it would make me really uncomfortable when I'm buying from someone who doesn't know what they're talking about. I would have always loved to have that tech understanding because when you have those cringey moments when you look back on deals that you feel like you could have won, there are certain questions that I knew flew over my head due to a lack of understanding of products.'

Rusty Branch, President, Compass Law Group, truly owns his niche:

'If you're starting to work for me and you want to open up Atlanta, no problem. There are 1,876 partners in Atlanta. I need you to memorise all of them. Know their names, know their birthdays, reach out to them – because what we're doing is we're calling those 1,876 people every year and saying, "Hey, I know the last eighteen years hasn't been your time to move. Does it make sense now?"'

KEY TAKEAWAY

Ultimately, you can choose to learn sales and have breadth of knowledge for a long time (lesson 68), but the most exceptional salespeople know their industry inside out as well.

Lesson 95: Prepare exceptionally to sell to senior people

How to think about prep

Dan Ingwell, Managing Partner, People Strategy Network, has a solid metaphor:

> 'The analogy of the professional sportsperson is a good one. The very best athletes train six days a week to play for ninety minutes, one day of the week. They train like hell on those six days; so in sales, why would you train for ten minutes or ten seconds before a call to do one of your five, ten or twenty most important meetings of the week?'

Richard Humphreys, ex-CEO, Saatchi & Saatchi, says:

> 'In the early days you could jump in the cab on a way to a presentation and make up most of what you were going to say on the spot. Those who really succeeded did a little more preparation, and that is certainly necessary these days. They think through what they are going to do just a little bit more. I still think too many people when they are selling just make the same presentations to everybody.'

Alexei Bezborodov, Commercial Director, Lux Research, tailors his prep levels to seniority:

> 'I prefer that level of preparation… Typically, what I see is that when I've prepared that way, even if I don't use any of the things that I've prepared, it

gives me really good confidence and I can speak about the things that are relevant to them. When I have that level of preparation, then that triggers ideas and allows me to take the conversation to a deeper level.'

When prep goes wrong

Anthony Charlton, Senior Manager, Gartner, has a preparation horror story:

'At one point, we had a CFO resignation, which clearly has an impact on a C-level executive. I remember walking up to a live meeting and just not having read about this event taking place at the beginning of the week, which clearly rocked the organisation, which meant that all the other prep was completely irrelevant to the conversation I was walking into. Not only is that incredibly embarrassing but it puts you in the most awful position. That is a hard way to learn – you need to have thorough preparation before walking into one of those situations.'

The upside of brilliant prep

Sugato Deb, Global Head of Sales Excellence, National Instruments, has sat on the other side of the table:

'I go back to my early experience developing products. When salespeople would come to me, I would ask myself, "Have you taken the time to understand the business and technical issues we face and how your product solves them?" If I don't have these questions addressed, then as a customer, I will need to put a lot of effort into figuring out if it'll really be useful… If the salesperson has taken the initiative and picked up on most of our issues, then they're going to have a lot of credibility, and the assimilation will be faster and more valuable to me as a customer. When a seller puts themselves in the shoes of their customer, seeing the world through their eyes, the sales and revenue will follow.'

KEY TAKEAWAY

Call preparation enhances confidence, strong questioning (lesson 73), and allows you to play on a level with top executives. Know the answers to many questions in advance and hypothesise the ones you don't know – senior people will appreciate you having done your preparation.

Lesson 96: Quantify your selling value

Bring it back to the numbers

Raf Tristao, Head of Strategic Accounts, HG Insights, says:

'It's all about getting an understanding of the size of the problem. If you don't know if this is a $10k problem or a $10m problem, you don't know how you're going to sell something that's $100k. They'll be like, "Well, there's no way I'm going to pay this to solve the $10k problem." However, if I'm actually impacting $10m worth of problem, that's an easy choice.'

Show them the whole picture

Anne-Marie Lee, Senior Manager, Aviva Financial Advisors, says:

> 'What I try to do is to get them into those conversations, persuading them that they've never done it before, a "why don't we try and take a holistic view?" approach. Then, with as much information as they are comfortable sharing with me, I give them a snapshot of where they are now financially. I relate that to what are their goals, what are their concerns that they have for their families, for their children, for their future or that house that they want to buy? And then see whether they have enough, or if they're on track, or if they actually have a plan in place to achieve those targets that they have set.'

Rupert Warburton, CEO, Caffe Kix, says:

> 'I had a coffee wholesale business called Kix Coffee, which I did well from because I managed to

land a global supply contract for coffee beans with a major airline for their business lounges... The build-up to that was modelling up the entire UK coffee wholesale supply industry and seeing how opaque and inefficient it was. I had also modelled up factory economics of coffee and realised that this airline was paying twice as much as they should be for coffee that was half as good as it should be. I was effectively able to improve their value by a factor of four, which is a pretty compelling proposition. All you have to do is say, "I'm going to double your quality and halve your cost."''

Decision intelligence

Scott Roy, CEO, Whitten & Roy, teaches quantification as a product:

'DQ™ is decision intelligence. We believe that the job of a professional salesperson is to help clients make the best possible buying decision for themselves or their families or for their businesses. And the way you do that is by exploring two subjects, in this order: the first subject has two topics: the problem and the cost of the problem. First, you must uncover and dig into the problem the client has so that they understand it at a much deeper level than they had previously. After the problem is well understood by the client, it's time to estimate the cost of the problem in terms of time wasted, money, efficiency, sales, productivity, etc. It is best to monetise the problem because once a person understands it in money terms, it helps clarify immediately if the problem is worth solving. If the answer is no, then that's the end of the conversation. Why would you waste your time and theirs pitching a solution to a problem not worth solving? This helps you to "fail fast" and move on to other prospects who have problems worth solving.

'If the problem is worth solving, then you take on the second subject, which also has two parts: the solution, and the value of the solution. The solution is matching your service or product to the problems and needs to be uncovered and the value of the solution is the estimated value that is created in monetary terms. If that number is large enough to satisfy the client you probably have a deal, even if the client has to reach deeply into their pockets or find money elsewhere in order to pay for it.

'When our large corporate clients adopt DQ Sales® they typically notice several things: deals get larger, deals move faster and there is more certainty that deals will close.'

KEY TAKEAWAY

Quantification is tough – it requires challenging questions and rapport with the clients so they can answer them. However, if you can get to the true value of a problem (lesson 66), you can easily see whether the value exceeds the cost and, if so, drive towards the sale.

Lesson 97: Use NLP and self-talk

Defining NLP

NLP stands for 'neurolinguistic programming' and many interviewees referenced this in regard to both themselves and their clients. Jamie Badar, CEO, V2R, is a certified practitioner of NLP. He says:

> 'NLP is a science and [relates to] human behaviour. As sales is mostly about understanding the psychology of buyers and company cultures, it provides a significant advantage to understand some of the "human machinery" at play. A simple example would be when you listen to someone, you can start listening at a different level. It's not only listening to what they're saying but also listening to how they're saying it, and listening to what they're not saying as well. You're listening to their tonality, their reflection points. You're also looking at their body language. You're looking at eye movements, you're looking at breathing, you're also looking at their skin tone and how that changes through conversation. Then you want to get in tune with that as much as possible.'

External NLP

External NLP influences others and makes them feel comfortable. Brad Revell, Head of Digital, Infor, explains external NLP:

'Your standpoint is understanding what people are doing, how they're behaving, what do they really mean? They may be saying one thing but meaning another thing, both consciously and subconsciously. A really simple example is if someone says to you, "I feel this way." You know they're more of a feeling person rather than a thinking person then – more feeling, more gut. Would I go back and say, "I think you should go do this?" I wouldn't do that. I would say, "How do you feel about this? How would you feel if I went down that path?" It may sound really simple, but sometimes using those words has a subconscious impact that is far greater than you can possibly imagine.'

Internal NLP or self-talk

Many interviewees were true experts in self-control, discipline and self-talk. Lee McCroskey, speaker, trainer and coach, Southwestern Speakers, says:

'NLP is keen on selecting the words you use to describe your situation. People describe their lives as, "It is so crazy. My life is crazy." When you say that, the word paints an image in your mind and it typically reinforces what you do not want. No one wants insanity in their life, but they are describing their life as insanity. You can choose a different description for what you are experiencing. I think that makes a big difference, but people get stuck with the words they use.'

Ron Alford, senior partner, Southwestern Consulting, carefully observes his own self-talk:

'It's not beating yourself up when you make a mistake. It's like, "OK, I'm going to get better because of that," really noticing my words. If someone calls me and says, "Hey, how was your week last week?" I'll say, "Dude, I had a couple of health issues but I'm getting better." How I answer that question is incredibly important. Affirmations are what I say to myself and then what I say to you about myself.'

Josef Dvorak, Country Manager, SBR Consulting, explains:

'Self-talk is the little inner voice in your head. It's constantly going on for everyone and salespeople especially. It's extremely important and today just before I called in, I needed to work on it again. It is the difference between you looking at your phone and going, "I know I should call this guy, but actually, let's leave it for tomorrow," and actually picking up the phone and pressing the green button, which is the major difference between success and non-success in sales. You can always find a way, and you can always find an excuse. Another great example of how to distinguish between an average and a professional salesperson.'

KEY TAKEAWAY

The fact that how you talk to yourself and others affects your perception and success is unsurprising, but the science behind it is surprisingly developed and advantageous.

You can find more resources and courses on NLP at www.exceptionalsalescareer.com/resources.

Lesson 98: Work through referrals wherever possible

Why referrals?

A recent article by HubSpot reveals that 47% of top performers regularly ask for referrals, compared to 26% of non-top performers.[14] Venetia Paske, Principal Consultant, SBR Consulting, says:

'An immediate way to make that pain of cold calling go away is to have an introduction from a trusted third person. That reduces barriers straight away. It presents you as a trusted advisor more than an unknown. Otherwise, we cannot get away from people's perceptions of salespeople.'

---

14 Frost, A, '75 key sales statistics that'll help you sell smarter in 2020' [blog post], HubSpot (updated 20 December 2019), https://blog. hubspot.com/sales/sales-statistics, accessed 30 September 2020

Jason Dial, Chairman, LGFG Fashion House, says:

> 'You can still build a business cold calling and knocking on doors, but that is the hard way, and it is not getting any easier. In our business, we track this, and it takes 300 cold calls to get one client, or it takes ten referrals. Do you want to work thirty times harder and take thirty more calls to get to a single client? The metrics are unbelievable, but let's just put the emotion into it as well. Do you want to build a clientele through referrals where there is an inherent trust or do you have to go in and really prove yourself every time? If you get referrals, everything else will fall in place as long as you have the discipline to make the calls, go to appointments. Generally, you are excited to do so when you have got a bunch of appointments from referrals already.'

Joe Pallo, Founder and CEO, Sell Nothing, believes referrals are the biggest opportunity area for most salespeople:

> 'I find consistently when it comes to referrals, that we are all rookies. We say, "Yeah, I'd like to have a referral but it is too much trouble to ask. Never mind." If you take that one area and get it up on par with all the other sales skills, you and your business are going to grow. Referrals are given to people, not to your company. So, if you can establish a relationship where they like you, you should get referrals – but you need to ask for them.'

How to get referrals

Teresa Sproul, Sales Leader, Tom James, explains how she gets referrals:

> 'We have a three-step process. First you give them kind of a referral pitch, telling them the huge goals you're working on. Then you ask them who they know, and then the second step is going into questions. If they don't know anybody, asking, "OK, well, who's the tallest guy? Who's the guy that drives the nicest car? Who has a Bentley or a Ferrari?" It's the different ways to find these prospects that have a lot of money and can afford really high-end clothing. Then the third step is giving them a list of twenty guys that they might know that we do research on beforehand. I built my business off referrals. We're pretty well trained to come up with ten questions to generate referrals before you even meet the guy.'

Jason Dial, Chairman, LGFG Fashion House, always shares his vision and huge goals first to get a reaction and entice referrals from clients:

> '"Wow, I thought this guy was just selling suits, but he has got plans to change the world, it is pretty cool." That is how I would encourage people to ask for referrals, by sharing their vision first.'

A good set of referrals can quadruple your sales, as they did for Venetia Paske, Principal Consultant, SBR Consulting, in a previous job selling polymers:

'Knowing I had trust and rapport, I said, "By the way, I am still trying to meet quite a few people in the areas, is there anyone else you think I should speak to in the polymers area?" And he got out his phone, he just scrolled through his address book, and he gave me a name and I was like, "Great! Anyone else?" He goes, "Yep," and we just went from A through to Z. I did not rush him, and he just gave me name after name.'

KEY TAKEAWAY

Why would you want to make your life 30% harder? They require confident questions and preplanning but referrals can accelerate your sales growth from good to exceptional.

Lesson 99: Leverage tech and process improvements

Sales is changing

When I was at Gartner, we used an expression with the executives we sold to: 'The pace of change will never be as slow as it is today again.' This is certainly true of the pace of technological change in sales. Katrin Kiviselg, Partner, NorthStar Consulting, highlights some of the changes she is seeing:

'Some sales organisations are using completely different tactics for selling. They use automation for lead generation, which sales organisations have never done previously. You can get off the wagon of change really fast. You need to be listening to young salespeople and you'll be surprised about how smart they really are.'

Lars Tewes, Director, Clean Living International, says:

'If you think about twenty years ago or even ten years ago, Excel spreadsheets were about the best anyone would have, or bits of paper or goal cards. Now there are so many technical tools out there that all track what people do. I still do not feel most of them track the right things, but they do at least track data that can give a bit of analysis as to whether someone is following the right process.'

Kristel Tuul, Growth Marketer, Consultant, says:

'I am a big fan of automation and the scalability it brings. When I had my own tech startup, we used platforms and automation for outreach. You can put all of your emails in an application and create a series of email outreaches until someone replies. Another tool allows you to see the location and company of anyone viewing your website, which helps with the timing of our outreach. What will be possible in sales using technology is amazing.'

Avi Weisenberg, CRO and startup advisor, reflects on the benefits of technology:

'It's all about how you can execute better than everybody else and the technologies that are going to support you in doing that. If you are in an F-16 fighter-pilot jet, you have got your pilot vision, where all of the data is being thrown at you in real time. The technologies I work with aim to start adding that to the sales process.'

Stay ahead

Sugato Deb, Head of Sales Enablement, National Instruments, says:

'I would want you to aspire and say, "I want to be a next-generation salesperson." The reality is that the next generation thinks the future is already here, and a lot of top companies have already moved in that direction. If you are not aligned with that perspective, just rethink the best place for you to be in the future.'

KEY TAKEAWAY

Part of continual learning (lesson 68) is embracing the inevitable technology-led sales that is coming, and an exceptional salesperson will be a next-generation one. For a list of specific technologies recommended by our interviewees, go to www.exceptionalsalescareer.com/resources.

Lesson 100: Thank customers and treat them well

Thank your customers

The best salespeople I interviewed made a point to thank their prospects and clients. JT Olson, CEO, Both Hands, says:

> 'Recognition is the cheapest form of motivation. If you recognise people for what they've done, it makes them feel good. I think any investment, whether it's time, a gift or anything else a person gives, deserves some form of appreciation and a thank you. You can send out newsletters to go to everybody, but I honestly think that the personal touch, where someone actually takes the time to say thank you, is invaluable.'

Jason Dial, Chairman, LGFG Fashion House, has learned from experience:

> 'I have not thanked clients, and they have gone away quietly. I have thanked clients, and they have championed my calls, so they become advocates when you express gratitude. People do not remember what you said, but they always remember how you made them feel.'

Treating people well

Ron Alford, Senior Partner, Southwestern Consulting, says:

> 'The more they start talking and opening up, they start letting out little pain points, and if I can find those pain points of course I compliment them, like, "Dude, it sounds like you're doing an awesome job, I love how you're in the trenches, I love hearing about your vision."'

Robin Mukherjee, MD, 2Circles Consulting:

> 'Being great at sales, it's like driving a really fast racing car, with lots of power. You have to treat the sales process with a lot of respect, otherwise the end results will not match your principles. It's really important that you do keep those principles and those philosophies, so you can stay on course, not lose control and treat people well. That's what makes your career long-term, healthy and fulfilling.'

Rusty Branch, President, Company Law Group, believes that sincerity is best:

> '[I say,] "Hey, one deal is not going to change my lifestyle. If it makes sense, I'm the happiest for you. If it doesn't make sense, we're going to high-five at the end of this." I think it absolutely gives me a competitive advantage knowing how to create a sincere buying atmosphere.'

The interviewees that I thanked and followed up with certainly gave me a disproportionate number of referrals and were much happier to hear from me, sometimes up to eighteen months after our initial interviews, than the ones I didn't remember to thank.

KEY TAKEAWAY

Thanking clients, mentors and other stakeholders in your lives has an outsized effect on your mutual happiness, the strength of your relationships, and ultimately, your sales.

Bonus lesson 101: Become recession-proof

Becoming exceptional in sales is a sure way to make yourself recession-proof. If I had the ability to place this book in twenty-year-old Jamie Hamer's hands (and somehow force him to read it), it would have saved learning these lessons the hard way, many times over. I hope it can provide some of that guidance for you.

While I have done everything possible to make the language and lessons in this book timeless, it is difficult to ignore the timings under which it was written, during the first of what I hope will be the only pandemic in our lifetime. Many of the later interviews from this project were coloured by COVID-19 commentary but the prevailing thoughts emphasised by many interviewees focused on finding great new roles and getting promotions.

In terms of final thoughts, I recommend going back to the beginning and considering why you might want to be in sales (lesson 1) and how you might get started (lesson 23). A day of planning and reflection can save you a huge amount of wasted effort in the long run, a lesson emphasised by many of our interviewees in considering what they would have done differently in their otherwise fantastic careers.

Thank you, dear reader, for investing your valuable time in reading this book. I hope these lessons have an outsized effect on your future exceptional selling performance. You can continue your learning, as well as read or listen to each of the 100+ interviews in full, at www.exceptionalsalescareer.com.

Acknowledgements

Twenty-two months and at least 110 interviews later (underpinned by hundreds of approaches and interview edits), I have a lot of people to thank. Clearly, the interviewees themselves, who will also be celebrated through the publishing of their wisdom at www.exceptionalsalescareer.com and on social media. I should also thank my editing team – close friends and freelancers – and my publishers at Rethink Press. First and foremost, however, I am grateful for everything I learned and experienced, and the amazing people I met, throughout this two-year process.

Many thanks especially to those who worked directly on this project: Funmi, Kristi, Denee, Iain and Maxi, Evan, and especially Rupa.

The Author

Jamie Hamer has had a diverse and impactful dozen years in sales, entrepreneurship and commercial strategy, and looks forward to continuing to learn from the best and deliver exceptional results.

His first job, while at university, was deeply formative, as he decided to travel from the UK to the USA to sell educational books door-to-door as an independent contractor with Southwestern Advantage, the oldest direct selling company in America. Working eighty hours per week, Jamie was the number one first-time European Salesperson (out of around 800). For his second summer, he recruited a team of five, increased his business value by 90%, and was the top second-year salesperson in the European organisation.

He then went on to a corporate career, beginning with five years at industry giant Procter & Gamble, where he won awards for his work on the Aussie, Wella, Duracell, Daz, Oral B, Pampers, and Iams brands, and was nominated for the 'Spirit of CBD' – the top sales award in the UK organisation. He then worked for two further market-leading organisations – the Acuris Group and Gartner – being nominated for the top account manager award at both, before starting his entrepreneurial journey.

Seizing on a market opportunity to start a business with three prolific journalists, Jamie now runs sales, commercial strategy, operations and finance for React News, which has grown to be a business with almost £2m in revenue and fourteen employees, and Europe's best-read paid real-estate news service, all within eighteen months of launch.

Jamie is also an accomplished public speaker (having been president of Holborn Speakers Toastmasters Club), a keen singer, and a tennis and basketball player. He holds a CFA Charter, which involved a gruelling study schedule of more than 1,000 hours to obtain.

Blessed with fantastic mentors and keen to repay their generosity whenever possible, Jamie is passionate about sales theory and process, which is the genesis of this project.

You can connect with Jamie at:

🌐 www.exceptionalsalescareer.com

🔗 www.linkedin.com/in/jamie-hamer-156a4328

Lightning Source UK Ltd.
Milton Keynes UK
UKHW022106290121
377893UK00008B/241